LAURA HERSHEY

ON THE LIFE & WORK OF AN AMERICAN MASTER

Edited by Meg Day and Niki Herd

ISBN: 978-0-9970994-4-7

Published by Pleiades Press & *Gulf Coast* & *Copper Nickel*

Department of English   Department of English
University of Central Missouri   University of Houston
Warrensburg, Missouri 64093   Houston, Texas 77204

Distributed by Small Press Distribution (SPD) and to
subscribers of *Pleiades: Literature in Context* and
Gulf Coast: A Journal of Literature and Fine Arts.

Series, cover, and interior design by Martin Rock.
Cover photograph courtesy of the Denver Public Library.

2 4 6 8 9 7 5 3 1
First Printing, 2019

The Unsung Masters Series brings the work of great, out-of-print, little-known writers to new readers. Each volume in the series includes a large selection of the author's original writing, as well as essays on the writer, interviews with people who knew the writer, photographs, and ephemera. The curators of the Unsung Masters Series are always interested in suggestions for future volumes.

Grateful acknowledgements to Robin Stephens and the Denver Public Library for permission to use the poems in this volume. Robin Stephens and the Denver Public Library retain the rights to Laura Hershey's poetry. No poems in this volume may be reproduced without their written permission.

Invaluable financial support for this project has been provided by the National Endowment for the Arts, the Cynthia Woods Mitchell Center for the Arts, and the Missouri Arts Council, a state agency. Our immense gratitude to these organizations.

National Endowment for the Arts
arts.gov
ART WORKS.

Missouri Arts Council
The State of the Arts

cynthia woods mitchell center for the arts
UNIVERSITY of HOUSTON

LAURA HERSHEY

ON THE LIFE & WORK OF AN AMERICAN MASTER

OTHER BOOKS IN THE UNSUNG MASTERS SERIES

THE UNSUNG MASTERS SERIES

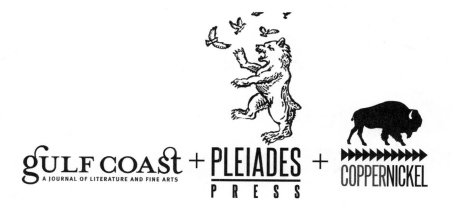

gulf coast
A JOURNAL OF LITERATURE AND FINE ARTS

+ PLEIADES
P R E S S

+ COPPERNICKEL

CONTENTS

SELECTED PROSE

PHOTO GALLERY

ESSAYS ON LAURA HERSHEY

INTRODUCTIONS

"STAIRS START TO CRUMBLE ALL OVER AMERICA WITH THE SCRATCHING OF A PEN": HONORING LAURA HERSHEY

On the night I was supposed to meet Laura Hershey for the first time, she was a no-show.

We had corresponded for a handful of years—brief, lively transmissions about disabled poets or ADAPT paperwork, accessible MFAs—and I'd wrung my hands in anticipation since Lambda Literary Foundation's press release announced our names together in the 2010 class of Emerging Writer Fellows. As is so often the case when we come up without access to our own lineages, I knew little of Laura Hershey's life, the expansiveness of it, and the great extent to which the work she'd done in the world had made much of my life—especially my education— possible. Whatever respect and recognition I lent Hershey at the time now seems trivial in comparison to her actual contributions. Hershey was a nationally recognized activist in the disability community, campaigning to increase the visibility of Deaf and disabled LGBTQ folks; to protect Deaf and disabled women from becoming domestic violence statistics; to eliminate work disincentives from social security; to increase independent living; to promote Medicaid home and community-based services; and to protect the rights of home care workers and assistive attendants. She was critical in the direct-action movements that led to accessible public transportation, interpreters and attendants in mainstreamed public schools, and the signing of the Americans with Disabilities Act in 1990.

But what I knew of her that night in Los Angeles was simple and life-giving: Laura Hershey was the first out queer disabled poet I'd ever read on paper. Though our experiences of disability and gender differed greatly, hers were the first poems where I witnessed my own multiplicity coalesce in English. It's easier for me now—though still not easy—to imagine a future as a disabled, queer activist and poet; at the time—and in these times—any one of those identities could get a person killed. Looking around, one might think that surely the combination of them already had. And yet: Laura Hershey.

We learn early that erasure, both literal and figurative, is one of the more vicious and duplicitous tenets of ableism— discrimination, violence, and social prejudice committed against disabled individuals and communities in order to protect and center the nondisabled. The more difficult it is to locate evidence of an experience, the more convincing its nonexistence, its irrelevance. The contemporary eugenics movement, in all its shifty iterations, has made it easy for nondisabled folks to rationalize the exclusion of disability. When Laura Hershey didn't show up that night, I worried. One Lambda fellow shrugged at her absence, suggested she might've changed her mind about attending. Disabled folks know better. We knew immediately who in the room was kin because we all shifted, re-evaluated the width of the door, mentally scanned the evening for stairs.

The next morning, the email arrived: Problems with travel. Lost luggage, lost tech. Missing piece of ventilator equipment. No local replacements. Resting. Send the assignment and see you later.

That afternoon in workshop, Laura Hershey took us to the mat.

> The poet in me wants
> to be out there, beyond the pane
> with the other poets.
> The poet in me wants
> to meet and greet,

get my gay on,
shine my wit, my stories:
    march of buoyant wheeling protests around
    marble departments;
    songs on long bumpy bus rides from Beijing to
    muddy Huairou.[1]

I remember clearly the feeling in the room. Hershey sat reading at one end of the long seminar table, while another eight of us flanked its sides evenly, holding our breath.

Imagine friendship incubated in deep reserves
of stamina and eloquent gesture.
Imagine so much lung capacity
you can afford to burn some of it away
in loud laughter and tobacco leaf.
Imagine writing about reliable bodies
striding unpaved rocky terrain,
and coupling toward revolution.[2]

Some of us shifted uncomfortably in our seats. A few of us grinned. Game on.

I'd never before been in a workshop with another proudly out disabled poet. I had no aptitude for it and reached or retreated in inconsistent ways, uncertain of how to ally without undercutting, champion without projecting. I had spent so much of graduate school defending the disability and Deafness in my work that I had little idea of how to critically celebrate and tend it when there was more than one of us at the table. Hershey's poems were bold, audacious, uncompromising. She wrote candidly about ableism, about queer crip sex and desire, and about the thorny wonder of having recently finalized the adoption of a teenager with her partner of twenty years, disabled activist and lawyer, Robin Stephens. Hershey modeled how to take up space without apologizing, how to make disability the given and not the exception. Hershey was as much about using a poem to tell

a story that could shut down a room as she was about knowing
when and how to use a body to shut down traffic, legislators,
violations of her rights. Her poems were sharp and witty and
never took themselves too seriously.

> Better yet, see me now!
> See me block this doorway, plant my wheels firm,
> see me lock my brakes!
> No, I tell some bureaucrat
> who wants to get into his office
> so he can make decisions about my future.
> No, I will not turn
> I will not move over
> I will not get out of your way
> not until the police order me to, under threat of arrest
> and maybe not even then![3]

Hershey was equally ruthless in her evaluation of poems, and
for the first time in my life I felt the intimidation and honor
and motivating drive nondisabled poets must feel all of the time
in workshop when other nondisabled peers validate their work,
understand its hiccups, or can locate the place where the volta
needs shifting because they're not so preoccupied with trying
to understand why deafness might find itself inside an ode to
joy. Hershey was generous and patient as an editor, but obdurate
too about the stakes. Does your poem inch us toward some kind
of liberation? Does your language obscure the path? Have you
thought recently about the ableism in belittling a poem by calling
it "accessible"? I keep Hershey's questions close.

Our workshop pulled two-a-days, swiftly gelling as a
cohort of poets who would and have continued to support one
another for the next decade. Near the end of the week, a poem
in our workshop used deafness as a metaphor to describe the
compulsory closeting many queer folks experience in their youth.
As the poet read, Hershey and I wordlessly locked eyes, blinked

knowingly, and went back to the poem. I have known butch nods in my life; I can spot a feminist snap[4] from across a crowded conference room with ease; but never have I felt the kind of relief in witness and solidarity as finally looking up from a poem while enduring its ableism to find kinship staring back. We tag-teamed the audism out of that poem, workshopped it gently and with the compassionate rhetoric trained into us as a part of queer crip survival and activism in the spaces we call home. Later in the courtyard, as the Los Angeles smog drained of color, Hershey and I chuckled about it, coined the look we'd shared a *crip sip*. "You can't drink too long," Hershey joked, "or else you'll be quenched enough to say what really needs saying." We sat a long time together without talking that night. We agreed to save the sharp edges for our poems.

When Hershey wrote and spoke about her relationship with Robin Stephens, she entered a new register. Sometimes it made us blush. Hershey's love poems are earnest without dipping into sentimentality and they preserve the presence and sexuality of disability without making it a spectacle for the nondisabled gaze. "How did you do that?" I'd asked her after workshop one day. I had few examples of how to write about queer crip desire outside of an ableist framework and Hershey's workshop poem about her spouse had left me flushed and emboldened. She frowned, asked who I was reading. "Why aren't you reading Constance Merritt?" she asked. "We're your family tree. We know how to love ourselves and others at the same time." In a Hershey poem, the addressee seems always to be a beloved—even when the beloved is the poet or disability or protest itself. For this reason, I find Hershey's love and lust poems thrillingly queer; they allow the personal to be political while still finding ways to separate the two when desire demands it. Laura Hershey was the first person in my life to tell me I could support something politically and choose to defy it in my personal life if I so wished. She drew a line between being publicly invested and privately desirous. As an elder, she gave me permission to imagine a different trajectory for my life; for the first time, it could include flexibility, forgiveness, and moments of rest, even if rest meant assimilation or a break from the cause.

> privately
> I do not care what it will cost
> to break these chains
>
> privately
> I am not thinking of the small business owner
> or his congressional representative
> or this smile-clad aide
>
> privately
> I am thinking of
> my lover
>
> myself and
> my lover[5]

In this way, Hershey's poems work to teach a sustainable practice of loving and fighting. She honored the difficulty of living in an ableist society while allowing herself to find pleasure and praise in the beauty that surrounded it. As in all her poems, Hershey insists that nothing is expunged, even the admission of what might seem to align with a medicalized view of a disabled life:

> I dream
> of pain too
> not the always ache
> of emptiness
> but full pain
> new pain
> yes
> I dream
> of happiness
> and

I dream
of pain too[6]

I have to assume Hershey took to her activism with at least as much boldness and ease of spirit. At the end of our week together, she popped back on a plane across the country to a radio interview about protesting the Muscular Dystrophy Association's annual telethon. When Hershey writes about her transition from MDA poster child and one of Jerry's Kids to an active member of Jerry's Orphans and the protests that refused the nation's pity, I feel in awe of the lives this poet lived. In her archive at The Denver Public Library's Western History Collection, I read the hate mail she received for protesting Jerry Lewis and his telethon; I read her measured and personal responses, her passionate arguments for reason and respect.

I read her correspondence about the two U.N. World Conferences on Women she attended, including events in Nairobi, Kenya, in 1985, and in Beijing, China, in 1995. I read the score for "You Get Proud by Practicing," set to music by the Kardon Institute for Arts Therapy. I read the invitation to the 1990 signing of the Americans with Disabilities Act and then I read President Clinton's remarks made during the 1998 President's Award ceremony at the White House. I read her acceptance speech for an honorary doctorate from her alma mater and the description of her unceasing labor on behalf of the human rights of disabled and marginalized women worldwide when she was nominated posthumously to the Colorado Women's Hall of Fame. I read the children's book she wrote. I reread *Survival Strategies for Going Abroad: A Guide for People with Disabilities*, a book that nearly saved my life a few years ago from a small hospital in Sliema, Malta. I read the arrest records and the letters to senators and the petitions for public apology.

And then I read her last letter to me, dated October 2010, one month before she died unexpectedly. We were designing a two-sided letterpress broadside of a pair of her poems, "Unanswered," and "Under the Super Shuttle Sign," a tongue-twister both of us agreed our speech therapists, though twenty years apart, would have appreciated. In the email, Hershey included a draft of her newest work, a longer piece of poetic prose called, "Remember." I keep this excerpt above my desk and next to a photo of the nine of us, grinning and green and not one bit erased.

> Remember, you're unabridged, strictly scrutinized, equally protected. Your personhood is legally recognized, but nowadays so is a corporation's. Remember when corporations prospered through good customer service? Remember, human nature is a myth but human rights are universal. Liability is an excuse; safety is a science. Remember to use the right lingo for each argument. Remember all the excitement when the bill was signed, the soaring promises? Remember, that doesn't apply here. Still, it's good to remember you belong here with the middle managers and the returning Disneyland disciples; you can't ask for a lot but you can ride along.

> Remember Bob Sampson on the Telethon? Remember who your friends are. From either left or right, if it stays clear we should be able to see the Grand Canyon. Remember, you're the seventh generation, and the keeper of one more. Remember, you're a charter member, a metropolitan citizen, a live birth, a party to the contract. Remember, what's starting here started long ago.[7]

—Meg Day

NOTES

1. Draft of "Loyalty," Laura Hershey Papers, WH2274, Box 8 FF4, Western History Collection, The Denver Public Library.
2. Ibid.
3. Laura Hershey, *In the Way: ADAPT Poems* (Denver: Dragonfly Press, 1992), 2.
4. Sara Ahmed, "Feminist Snap," *Living a Feminist Life*, 2017.
5. Untitled draft, Laura Hershey Papers, WH2274, Box 3 FF32, Western History Collection, The Denver Public Library.
6. Draft of "Pain, Too - 1987," Laura Hershey Papers, WH2274, Box 3 FF32.
7. Laura Hershey, "Remember," Email, 2010.

THE GROUNDWORK FOR A MOVEMENT: POET AND DISABILITY ACTIVIST LAURA HERSHEY

It seems appropriate to begin the conversation of Hershey's life as an activist poet in the context of two major civil rights laws: the Civil Rights Amendment of 1964 and the Americans with Disabilities Act of 1990. The 1964 amendment is significant as Hershey's birth two years prior ushered her into a culture where racial bias was cemented into its very landscape. Though aware of her own white privilege, it was in this tenuous racial landscape of the 60s and 70s, with its nonviolent protests and radical proclamations of black empowerment, that Hershey would come to find parallels between the struggles of black citizens and those disabled. While there was no signage stating "Able-Bodied Only," the manifestations of disability segregation and discrimination were everywhere. An Arapahoe County School District letter, dated 1967 and addressed to Evelyn Hershey, describes the younger Hershey as different from "the normal kindergarten children"[1] with whom she would be attending school. The letter was penned in a tone barely hiding the county's disdain for educating a child with disabilities. In societal shunning, segregated housing and educational spaces, and disability eugenics, Hershey found parallels between the oppression of black citizens and the disabled; and with those parallels, she borrowed similar strategies from the Civil Rights Movement for her own activism. Tactics, such as her insistence upon non-violent protest, resembled Martin

Luther King's. In her archive, there are sticky notes reminding protesters to remain peaceful. But the tone of her activism, and the work drawn from it, is much more like Malcolm X's. She had the courage of both civil rights leaders.

Hershey made sure her voice was heard when she and her comrades held up traffic with wheelchairs demanding access to transportation in downtown Denver. There's a plaque just a block or so from her archive commemorating the moment. Hershey had the audacity to challenge every television viewer, like myself, who tuned in yearly to watch the Jerry Lewis Muscular Dystrophy Telethon. Hershey fought, domestically and internationally, for the freedom of disabled people, and did so understanding long before it was a buzz word, the importance of intersectionality. Two years after the passage of the Americans with Disabilities Act, speaking of the ways in which the disabled community is defined, Hershey located struggle in the context of the black, Jewish, and LGBTQ communities, as a defining trait and a unifying factor amongst oppressed peoples:

> We have shared, if not identical, experiences of segregation and exclusion. At one time or another, most of us have found ourselves, sometimes willingly but usually unwillingly, separated from the mainstream of society. This segregation may take the form of back entrances to buildings, "special" transportation, sheltered workshops, separate classrooms, or nursing homes. These experiences of segregation may be temporary and minor, or lifelong and spirit-crushing."[2]

In 1983, Hershey spent a year abroad in England on a Watson Fellowship. There she researched disability culture with a special interest in issues concerning women. She returned to the states working on behalf of women locally and domestically by co-founding the Denver chapter of Handicapped Organized Women and the Domestic Violence Initiative for Women with

Disabilities. In her introduction to *Flights: Poems of the Beijing Women's Conference 1995*, Hershey speaks of her beginning interest in international disability issues and the ways in which her poetry is in conversation with that work:

> In 1985, I embarked on a journey into an international community of strong resilient women—my sisters with disabilities around the world. My journey began in Africa, at the Non-Governmental Organization (NGO) Forum on Women in Nairobi, Kenya. I did not know then that, ten years later, my journey would take me to Asia.... In between, women with disabilities emerged as a force to be reckoned with in our communities and countries.... These poems grew out of that energy, and they are dedicated to those women.[3]

Commitment to the disability community reflected itself in Hershey's poems a myriad of ways. At the World Conference on Women in Beijing, the poet and her partner, Robin Stephens, produced a brief print and oral history project focusing on the leadership needs of disabled international women. Nicaraguan Petrona Benita Sandoval was one conference participant whose story made it into Hershey's poetry. In a poem simply titled "Petrona," Hershey uses source texts to articulate one woman's tenacity in providing resources to other women living with disability due to war:

> "The men said
> that because we weren't veterans,
> we didn't have the right
> to participate
> in the organization."[4]

As is common in Hershey's work, the first-person point-of-view collapses between poet and subject matter, in this case Petrona, with only quotation marks reminding the reader who is the speaker at any given moment. The poem's use of documentary techniques, with its focus on Nicaragua, brings to mind the work of Ernesto Cardenal. Hershey would later return to the work of oral history, documenting important figures in disability rights history for the Bancroft Oral History Project at Berkeley.

Poems like "Translating the Crip" and "You Get Proud by Practicing," among Hershey's more recognized works, are purposefully didactic and written in plain speech. There is nothing academic about the work, if academic means a level of inaccessibility. The three poetry chapbooks in her archive illustrate this point well. *In the Way* (1992), *Dreams of a Different Woman* (1994), and *Flights* (1997) were all produced on copy machines with bright-colored cardstock for covers. The cover of *In the Way* depicts the image of a stick figure in a wheelchair breaking free from chains. The poems in that particular chapbook were directly inspired by Hershey's work advocating for attendant services and independent disabled living. As was the case for many women poet activists writing during Hershey's time—feminists such as Audre Lorde or Minnie Bruce Pratt—poetry was not simply art; it served the utilitarian purpose of progressing the goals of a particular movement or cause—that of sisterhood, black empowerment, lesbian rights, etc. But as strong and commanding as Hershey's voice is in her activist poems, the body of her work illustrates a tone and color far from being monochromatic. In these poems, some written in traditional forms, about loss, landscape, or sexual desire, the reader is privy to a narrator/poet with a keen sense of observation; these poems are slow, quiet, vulnerable, and existential. These poems refuse relegation to any kind of box.

In the poem "Flights," Hershey writes about the toll of activism in the struggle against "design apartheid,"[5] stating that "[s]tairs are no longer poetic."[6] Hershey's archive is filled with letters, written some fifteen years after passage of the Americans with Disabilities Act, to politicians documenting her inability to "fully participate in the Democratic process" because many precincts were built with only stairs or narrow entryways

Hershey's archive in Denver is sizable. It is divided into several series and includes more than thirty boxes of disability pamphlets and magazines from the 1980s up to Hershey's death in 2010. The archive contains completed grant applications, correspondence from Jerry Lewis, permits for the "Tune Out Jerry" campaign and other protests. There are hundreds of letters from congressmen and other officials pertaining to the passage of the ADA; there is an equal number written to address the need for continual ADA oversight and accountability. There is a 1991 *Denver Post* article with a headline calling the ADA a "nightmare" for senior citizens. The article paints the picture that allowing the disabled equal access to housing will leave elderly citizens open to increased violence and crime. That narrative—fear of the other— felt familiar to me. It's this familiarity, and those connections Hershey makes between black oppression/black empowerment and disability oppression/disability pride, that drew me to this project and to a poet I didn't know previously. And the fire in her poems, the enormity of her activism and its reach, raises the question why her work has remained unsung. Had Hershey accepted her admission into Harvard or Princeton, would that life choice have given her poetry the credentials, at times required, to make it worthy of consideration and critical thought, thus allowing for a wider audience? I don't know the answer to this question, or whether Hershey would think it important. We can be certain, however—with current policies geared towards gutting healthcare for those who need it most, increasing hostility towards the LGBTQ community, and a president who mocks disabled people on national television—that the current moment is a facsimile of the 60s and 70s. As such, attention to Hershey's work is needed more than ever.

—Niki Herd

NOTES

1. Arapahoe County School District to Evelyn Hershey, Laura Hershey Papers, WH2274, Western History Collection, The Denver Public Library.

2. Laura Hershey, Crip Commentary: Selected Denver Post Opinion-Editorial Columns (Denver: Dragonfly Press, 1995), 4-5.

3. Hershey, Laura, *Flights: Poems of the Beijing Women's Conference 1995* (Denver: Dragonfly Press, 1997), i.

4. Ibid., 8.

5. Rob Imrie,. "Oppression, Disability and Access in the Built Environment" in *The Disability Reader*, edited by Tom Shakespeare (London: Continuum, 1998), 129.

6. Laura Hershey, *Dreams of a Different Woman: New Poems* (Denver: Laura Hershey, 1994), 37-38.

A NOTE ABOUT THE TEXT

Many of the poems in this volume originally appeared in multiple drafts across various mediums. Handwritten, dictated, typewritten, word processed, audio recorded, video-recorded, carbon-copied, and emailed poems in Hershey's oeuvre often included at the bottom of the text the year in which each was written. While this was especially useful in locating the most recent version of each poem, we have removed these dates for uniformity in reading. Given the extensive nature of Hershey's papers in the Denver Public Library's archive, her abundance of self-distributed poetry chapbooks and pamphlets, and Hershey's own practice of sending—through post or email—early drafts of unpublished poems, establishing an accurate chronology for these poems seemed not only challenging, but disingenuous. We have opted instead to retain the capitalization, spelling, line alignment, and punctuation of the most recent drafts available. Due to the evolution of Hershey's disability—and the ways in which the progression of technology and the cooperation of attendants shifted over time to provide or deny particular kinds of access—we have chosen not to enforce an ableist poetics via copyediting, even and especially when technology or dictation assistance might explain why such supposed idiosyncrasies occur.

POEMS

I Am, I Am Not

I am
a tributary, feeding the rapids of your guilt.
I am
an encyclopedia of answers
to your curiosity
about God, physiology, and toilets.
I am? I *am?*
No, I am not.
That is not why I'm here.

I am—you call me—
victim, suffered, patient.
I am—you see—
smiling tot begging money on TV;
state poster child 1973.
I am—you think—
confined, courageous
in stalwart opposition
to what my legs have fated.
I am? I *am?*
No, I am not.
I am not what you think.
I am not what you see.
I am not what you call me.

If Faith

A face never was as familiar or as friendly
as the moon's. Ninety degree nights she lit generously
giving me something of substance to pray to
as I never had.
Praying, this could be a problem. No bearded deity
earns my reverence,
no king of heaven gets my patronage
over the most ordinary bag lady.
But things happen.
Only six returns of that faithful moon
had brought me love, sex,
and near-death.
Some new awareness rooted in me, some appreciation
of how gratitude
and fear
combine to invent religion.
Perhaps I too knew this need, knew it
in my laughing heart, knew it
in my thankful flesh, knew it
in my aching chest.
If faith
could open my lungs
as it had opened two hearts—
then why not ask?
Vain coughs, a burning moon told me
to ask,
to embrace the unaccountable knowledge in my
    heart—

heart all around me,
spirit dwelling in touch,
divinity in my bones, in the food I ate, in the moon.

Remembering now
brings gratitude again, and the moon returns faithfully
like a mother
with the same inexplicable, heart-true message:
Be joyous.

Everything inside and outside disputes
this message. Self-conscious intellect will rule.
As always, what prevents the embrace
is shame.

In the Way

Could you move, the waitress says,
politely of course,
you're in the way.
A common request, my trusted wheelchair just
an impediment, an obstacle to the busy,
a clumsy roadblock I haul with me down every road
and when parked
an interruption
or at least a slowing down
of the life I only
wish to be part of; a piece of surplus furniture
in the already crowded rooms
of restaurants, bars, theaters.

Usually
I accommodate,
backing into corners
turning sideways
angling my wheels
to leave a clear path
asking, politely of course,
Is that better?

I get in the way
without trying.
I apologize
excuse myself
and move out of the way.

But not today.
Today I listen
to a small, recalcitrant voice inside
that insists:
*Such power
should not be wasted.*

If I alone can be so much
and so often in the way,
if I can create such worry among waitpersons
such consternation in concert halls
such alarm in the aisles
of grocery stores
just imagine the aggravation a dozen
or two dozen
or three hundred
people using wheelchairs can cause people
who would rather not see our needs
or hear our demands
or acknowledge our rights!
Just imagine!

Better yet, see me now!
See me block this doorway, plant my wheels firm,
see me lock my brakes!
No, I tell some bureaucrat
who wants to get into his office
so he can make decisions about my future.
No, I will not turn

I will not move over
I will not get out of your way
not until the police order me to, under threat of arrest
and maybe not even then!

In the way
in the way all day,
I woman this barricade which is mine
whenever I need it,
this roadblock I haul with me down every road,
this wall I can construct at will,
and be happily in the way with,
and say no with,
and plaster with scrawled signs about freedom,
and add to the bigger walls growing
around whole buildings, around whole city blocks.
I can turn back
customers, employees, delivery people, even cops.
I can keep the usually powerful
in or out of their offices.

I can be in the way
in the way
I can be in the way
my way.

Monster Body

I mock the human form, just missing those
    specifications
on which everyone agrees. I furnish nightmares with
    personnel
typecast to illustrate terrors: immobility; the
    randomness of damage.
I roar when burned by exile, the mob swinging angry
    torches through stone streets.
Dangerous until empathy repatriates me, I carry
secrets in my castle, fainted women in my healing
    search.

My back's shell-sharp curve, my thin wrist bone,
limbs that do not twitch beyond the digits;
right lung so different from left—the leader, thrust
    forward, fuller-breathed,
pushing against ribs; while its more delicate mate
    shrinks,
adjusts inside a smaller, collapsing cage—
my brief breaths, bent bones; muscles weak as water,
    still as sleeping stars.
Monster mine, monster body,
one I would not trade.
Not for gold, not for leading roles,
not for promise of perfection, the protection it affords.

Monster body mine:
Creation not of fevered literary imagination
nor science run amok.

Just parts made from imperfect materials:
sinew, scar, cells, fluid, fat, and heart.
Such is the shape I take, my body—

but the pronoun *my* distorts the relationship; the
    spaces
imply a separation that does not exist.
Have stands too distant.
MonsterBodyMine, instead—
this makes *am* true.
MonsterBodyMine
fills the screen with frail menace.
Flesh threat, stubborn vulnerability shocks like
    violence.

MonsterBodyMine.
With my body, in my body, as my body,
by my body I journey.
It is my medium for learning, for love.
It is my lens, my light.
MonsterBodyMine

Message

Sometimes I want to go back
four years
then return quickly
to now
having delivered
my message.

Sometimes I want to go back
to the woman I was then;
young, new to the battle but eager,
busy and bright,
not even aware of her own loneliness.

Sometimes I want to go back
to the Detroit road where,
marching with 60 others,
we introduced ourselves between chants.
I want to follow alongside,
follow my young-woman-self's gaze
as it followed you, her new friend.

Sometimes I want to go back
in some form—
whispering bee,
bright neon sign—
whatever would attract my
or her attention away from you
for five seconds—

whatever would convey this good news
most effectively.

Sometimes I want to go back
and tell her
something
I hope she'll remember
in the months and years to come:
the times together
and the times apart,
the times of shared adventure,
the times of longing,
the times of terrible pain
as she becomes
aware of her own loneliness.

Sometimes I want to go back
and tell her
as exclamation,
as reassurance,
as gospel,
as balm:

> "Someday this woman—
> this beautiful woman—
> someday this woman
> will be your lover."

Lunch Break

Mid-afternoon, clouds have gone away,
as every July day, for a few hours,
in Nairobi.
Women all around:
in circles, singing
the rich-rhythmed songs of tribes combined;
in groups, dancing
bright clothes, muscled bodies flow;
in pairs, talking
musical and articulate as all the voices
of birds;
in solitude, listing,
watching the rest
in wonder.

I'm with Sharon, my English friend, sharing
a sandwich and Pepsi.
We don't need to talk
as she holds the food to my mouth
and bends the straw
for my drinking;
so we listen
to the variegated chorus
of chant, question,
planning, laughter, song,
and stumbling translation
around us.

An American woman approaches me,
camera in hand.
I have seen her, these few days,
snapping the heads and faces
of African women who,
I've noticed,
often frown for their portraits.

"Mind if I take your picture?" she asks.
"Alright," I answer.
She steps back, angles
her camera from a distance, the focus
on my wheelchair—
metal frame, shortened leg rests, torn green upholstery,
large tread tires—
then she waits.
We wait too, casually posed
under the hot sun. To Sharon she says,
"Will you give her another bite?"
"No," I snap. "Get this over with."
Her face changes, as if
I had spoken the language
of the Maribou stork.

How did this happen?
Am I a curiosity
to my own countrywoman?
So be it.

I will join the gallery
of those captured in the photographer's empty frame
and bare vision—
the Masai, Luo, Kikuyu
the Navajo, Pueblo, Sioux
the Amish
the Eskimo, the gypsy
the children
the old, the dark, the poor
the Native Islander, the Oriental
and "Woman"—
not born exotic,
but made so
by collectors' frozen images.

And in these frames, these photographs
of random, nameless faces,
we all know why
so many of us
are frowning.

Insomnia

While you sleep, I stir
the stew of our late night spat,
polish a pea of gravel stuck
in our sock-like fit.
I wail, rail at you
to rewrite the fight, dislodge the grudge
with tender apology.
On your side, sleep has already
softened the stone to nothingness
but I hold tight to hurt
slicking it to pearl.

While you sleep, I stir
the rain-lush scent of lust satisfied
that's left me wide
open and astonished;
your soft breath-gusts
brush my upper arm,
replay our rhythm.
It's lullaby to you;
to me it's hullabaloo.

This is how we lie sleeping,
or waiting for sleep:
on your right side, my left;
arm over back, cheek under hand,
elbow against wrist, pulses joined,
a soft throb of connection that will last
until you turn over, or I do.

This is how we live: sleeping
seals the deals we make by light;
we neighbor our enfleshed bones
like poems bound by pages.

canyon

left and right   I divide
my surfaces   falling away
under your   trickle

already you   are like centuries
of spring   runoff
coursing   fingers finding

a route between   my banks
creating first   a stream
then a river   then

a canyon
I deepen   with every gush
widen or   narrow to hold your eddies

your circuitous   irresistible current
your slow melt   and your occasional
delightful   rapids

I teem   with chasms of air
rock   and hungry birds landing
searching   for nests

if some summers   the river
seeps a dusty trace my shores unwet
still   the canyon lives

Sentence

a sentence slips from me like silk
spun smooth raw-edged
unfolding now
between hidden lips
red banner spreading silk   message of
time passing
cradle rocking falling
power blood speaking

this is an easy birth
no contractions no knuckled screams

just quiet bursting forth
of roseflesh

though careless where my issue lands
graceless eloquent tissue
i revere the force it represents
respect the torrent scattering
my petals

overdue
overstaying welcome
mocking man's grid-block calendar
overpainting the lines

control
is out of the question
period

from dream into word
each shred emerges from larva
draws breath
palpitates free of this nutritious enclosure
bares shocking colors
crimson orange almost black
takes flight

I weaken
rejoice for
it is my blood filling these wings

Orion on the Porch

Three nickel-glint belt loops of Orion,
the moon his round shield, brighten and dim like
    swaggering Elvis neon.
The phenomenon has an undeniable particularity, the
blinking a closer
        source:

the motion-detecting floodlight on my own
    back porch.
As I lean back into night's iced air, as I let myself still,
the flashing too relaxes; electricity stops speaking;
    fires more real
flare louder, burn up hundreds of light-years' travel.
    I watch the void
become its full black self, unblurred by atmosphere or
    blood.
Last night—I missed it—this moon, this porch, this
    hemisphere
lay bathed in shadow, eclipsed at midnight, cleansed
    pure
as a candle; and today this porch, this house,
with a few strokes of ink, became mine

                  became ours.
You wait inside for me, in a room heated and lit, your
    warm body
somewhere between possibility and promise. Yesterday
    you brought
me roses. They droop their pink heads slightly, pray
for time to slow down. Our restless cat plays

around the vase, chewing and dancing in the grassy
    fountain.
I scarcely noticed all this before; but my appointment
with Orion on the dark porch, shortened by chill,
showed me what light can and can't reveal.

Delving

i.
Like a dream
I can't figure: stuck
in a hospital bed, sick
without symptoms.
Wearing white,
technicians come bearing trays
of needles, syringes; each tries
to locate the rich, secret
vein running deep in my bent arm.
Though grown, I scream a child's futile rage,
protective of my swaddled seam—surprised
then alarmed
when at last he stops, withdraws the clumsy lance,
the cold tingle that rends
my meshy tissue.

        Some other terror buds. I bid him start again.
For it wasn't pain, exactly, pried howls from my chest.
The needle's indifference hurts worse;

I can bear the numb discomfort
of clean metal spearing flesh.

ii.
Reconciled to the search, I still
my writhing senses and bastion voice.
Now my concentration urges

the tiny honed spear toward its mark.
Empty plastic puckers, pulls,
the way I would suck a turbid river
through a blind straw

awaiting sudden flood.
I am certain of the lode
but cannot map it for the awkward drill
delving sharpened arrow
tunneling through tendons and nerves.

In this dim, summarized white room, symptom
and shelter
of my imagination,

I wait, expecting scarlet gush,

as every month I yearn
to see my own blood.

iii.
But the syringe stays sterile.
The clumsy needle
can't quench my avid anticipation; the vein
remains buried in bone and fat,
a cache of riches, potent red life.

iv.
I'm left
finally
awake to ponder
dreamless
possible paths the needle misses
or wider openings
to that ruby wellspring—

and which side I am on
of these fought and delving searches.

We Weren't Carded

When we came in we weren't
carded, we rarely are, they're too
embarrassed:

For all they know
we could be sixty
or fourteen,
and either way would be a scene. We don't care, yet.
You and I both know
what doors guilt opens.

They won't guess our age
because they don't see our faces.

They see
tread tires and metal,
my bent back, your spastic arm,
the black plastic knobs that propel us.
they see the ten dollars
sent to last year's telethon and Heidi's
spiteful cousin.

all day i talk to my word processor

all winter is warmer
than a day
of sterile sunshine

      i pretend that the world is too loud   every
click roar jangle ssscrape hum or disproportionate
conversation
interrupts
my work. so that "alpha" sounds
in the interfering noise too much
like "papa"
and "word right" like "print"
and "repeat" like "delete"
repeat like delete
repeat like delete

this is how i work:

all day i talk to my word processor

The Gamble

We are taught not
to gamble.
Perhaps it is thought we have lost
enough already—legs, vision, speech,
the typical use
of our bodies.
Others' fears would teach us
to cringe at any thought
of any risk.
Disability and risk
don't mix.
Risk is something
we are supposed to be protected from—
by agencies, by professionals—
by parents, by doctors—
by invisibility,
by shame—
by confinement if necessary.
We must be kept safe: This is one of the lies
which fills the beds
of the so-called "homes."

So we embrace the risks
to fight the lies.

This is our gamble:

Minute by minute, city after city—
from the tense beginning to the jubilant or

scattered end
of every protest—
with every rhythmic word of every chant—
at each blocked entrance, each barricade—

with every defiant inch forward—
every move toward
freedom for our people—
any time we raise a fist
or a song
to mean
We're never going away—
in every confrontation, up and down the length
of the stand-off—
each and every time, we are
testing the humanity
of people who wear a badge,
carry a gun—
and fear our incomprehensible strength.

We know this is
a dangerous test—for some fail as extraordinarily
as others pass.
It is a gamble, risky and promising.
It may pay off
in unmet eyes or a curious stare,
surly dismissals or a question,
dialogue
or bruises.

Working Together

Her job: brisk bristle circle on teeth
My job: sneer
open wide

Her job: apply soap
loofah
hot spray
My job: how hot
say stop

Her job: heft my flesh
point a to point b
My job: remind her of our
respective spines and limbs

Her job: what no one thinks of doing
except for self or child
My job: make her forget
help her remember
tell her she can

Hate, But

I.

But perhaps I shouldn't call it hate.
Hate is not a word I would want to use
in those pleasant, lavender-filled bookstores,
those artsy cafes,
where I have managed to capture thirty ears,
an hour's attention,
to build a friendly bridge of words
between their reality
and mine.
I have come to think of each reading
as an opportunity, a promise
of sharing, and hearing,
and seeing,
as my audience adjusts its eyes
to the appearance of my body, my wheelchair,
and opens its mind anyway.
Hate is not a word
to present to such open minds.

I know this other word
and another, easier voice to talk about it with.
Ignorance.
Ignorance, then.
Let us talk
about ignorance.

II.
If I were here alone, I could have overlooked it.
I could have cheered with the rest
his verbal dexterity, his colorful, inventive tale,
could have disregarded the insults,
the sting of unfit words—
          "cripple" "inferior" "defective" "deformed"
used so easily.

I could have come away from his reading
not exactly inconspicuous—
my chair stalling a couple of times on the steep
          auditorium ramp—
not exactly belonging—
exiting the building by a separate, accessible door—
but sharing the group's satisfaction, a story told well.
But I am not here alone.
Two friends using wheelchairs, another with a white
          cane,
gather with me in the lobby,
out of the crowd's way.
Our frustration comes spitting out of each of us:
          "Jesus Christ" "I did not need this tonight"
          "How could he?"
          "At an AIDS benefit, of all things"
Bjo is shaking her head.
Robin wants to block his psychedelic bus,
          parked out front,
the way we did throughout the eighties,
before the federal mandate for accessible

transportation.
Mary looks close to tears.
I stare at the departing crowd,
white Eugene liberals and their bright children.
They are smiling six hundred smiles.
I wonder if they would have smiled
at a story sprinkled with "nigger" and "kike."

On one thing we all agree:
"It's just ignorance," we tell each other.
The same old shit. The same old ignorance.
Later I wonder:
Could the man who wrote *One Flew Over
    the Cuckoo's Nest*
be so ignorant?
It hits me that this ignorance—
If that's what it is—
is a battle I can't win.
Simple math shows why:
My own reading earlier the same day
my own effort to reach, to enlighten
drew an audience one-twentieth this size
or less.

III.
So if it is not just ignorance—
What can I call it?

What can I call the man who tells a radio host
how glad he is

that his daughter died young,
because she was in a wheelchair
and could not feed herself?

It is hard to call it hate
without the crimes we usually associate
with hate.

No one has ever leaned
from a passing car
to yell at me clear words of hate.
They do not scream out, calling me cripple or gimp,
they do not have to. Such words slip easily
from more respectable tongues.
They do not scream out, calling me dyke,
though as it happens, I am a dyke.
They do not scream out, calling me hag or bitch,
though as it happens, I am a witch.

They cannot imagine me being anything
other than what
they think they see.

They do not know who I am,
and this is the crime,
this is the violence.
This is the hidden hate
of which I do not want to speak.

the mom and pop print shop hop, or how eagles

how eagles
frozen and fierce
arched haughty judgment upon
weaker birds that flock
how their supposed virtue
hung silent bronze ascension

how engraved words
lectured from flag spangled
cork board walls
how exalted main street ambition scorned the knotty
nets of safety
and made need a sin

how among the order specifications he
asked
right between 20 pound and 24 pound
right between ember blue and ivory
how right out of ink stained
coffee filtered file cabinet air
how without pardon me
how without is this too personal
he asked
were you in an accident

how he pressed for what to call it
when I said all my life
how he flickered flat lipped regret
under eagles' yawning wings

and
how he tossed off
his granddaughter's story
how *can't do anything* sums her up
neater than tick tick rolling
out paper on his desk
how he answered all questions
with decisive negations
doesn't go to school
doesn't talk
can't do anything
oh every now and then you can see
there's something there
but
can't do anything

and especially
how he said
but she gets a lot
of attention

How to Write a Poem

Don't be brilliant.
Don't use words for their own sake, or to show
how clever you are,
how thoroughly you have subjugated them
to your will, the words.

Don't try to write a poem
as good as your favorite poet.
Don't even try to write
a good poem.

Just peel back the folds over your heart
and shine into it
the strongest light that streams
from your eyes, or somewhere else.

Whatever begins bubbling forth from there,
whatever sound or smell or color
swells up, makes your throat
fill with unsaid tears,

whatever threatens to ignite your hair, your eyelashes,
if you get too close—

write that.
Suck it in and quickly
shape it with your tongue
before you grow too afraid of it
and it gets away.

Don't think about
writing a good poem, or a great poem,
or the poem to end all poems.

Write the poem
you need to hear;
write the poem you need.

A Call to Arms

O bark the tree; leaf the book;
uncork the bottles, and stir the cook.
Winter the worn, torn calendar.
Spring the forgotten prisoner.
Breach all borders; stoke all hopes.
Quarter the soldier but disorder the troops.
Draft the breeze. Beam down the sun.
O pen your poetry, everyone.

Special Vans

The city's renting special vans,
the daily paper reads,
The cops are getting ready,
for special people with special needs.

The mayor's special crip advisor
has given special training
in moving all our special chairs
when arresting and detaining.

They've set up special jail cells
in a building on the pier.
They've brought in special bathrooms
and nurses—never fear.

They cops are weary of our bodies
they treat us in a special way,
special smiles, if you're lucky
special brutality when you're in the way.

Bush's campaign office gives us
all the special treatment we can take;
locked doors and angry words,
while Clinton's office gives us cake.

The ones who run the nursing homes
think they're doing noble deeds—
locking up our friends in cages
special people with special needs.

They put up special barricades,
to try to keep us out,
still we're in their face,
still we chant and shout.

What's so special really
about needing your own home?
If I need pride and dignity,
is that special, just my own?

Are these really special needs,
unique to only me?
Or is it just the common wish,
to be alive and free?

Telling

What you risk telling your story:
You will bore them.
Your voice will break, your ink
spill and stain your coat.
No one will understand, their eyes
become fences.
You will park yourself forever
on the outside, your differentness once
and for all revealed, dangerous.
The names you give to yourself
will become epithets.
Your happiness will be called
bravery, denial.
Your sadness will justify their pity.
Your fear will magnify their fears.
Everything you say will prove something about
their god, or their economic system.
Your feelings, that change day
to day, kaleidoscopic,
will freeze in place,
brand you forever,
justify anything they decide to do
with you.
Those with power can afford
to tell their story
or not.
Those without power
risk everything to tell their story
and must.

Someone, somewhere
will hear your story and decide to fight,
to live and refuse compromise.
Someone else will tell
her own story,
risking everything.

Note from Oregon

There's more shade here.
When the light doesn't fall
directly on a thing, sometimes I can see it better;
study its contours by the dark places in it.
Dreams grow like ferns
under the cover of denser forests.
The bottom of the sky is richer
and further away.

The river is loud.
Maybe it wants to silence me.
Not forever,
just a few moments,
so I'll stop and close my eyes
to hear
how different the current sounds
upstream, and down.

In the dark, the page stays clear
even as I write—
till I look, and something has come to life, whole,
under the branches.
There's more shade here.

You Get Proud by Practicing

If you are not proud
for who you are, for what you say, for how you look;
if every time you stop
to think of yourself, you do not see yourself glowing
with golden light; do not, therefore, give up on yourself.
You can
get proud.

You do not need
a better body, a purer spirit, or a Ph.D.
to be proud.
You do not need
a lot of money, a handsome boyfriend, or a nice car.
You do not need
to be able to walk, or see, or hear,
or use big, complicated words,
or do any of the things that you just can't do
to be proud. A caseworker
cannot make you proud,
or a doctor.
You only need
more practice.
You get proud
by practicing.

There are many many ways to get proud.
You can try riding a horse, or skiing on one leg,
or playing guitar,
and do well or not so well,

and be glad you tried
either way.
You can show
something you've made
to someone you respect
and be happy with it no matter
what they say.
You can say
what you think, though you know
other people do not think the same way, and you can
keep saying it, even if they tell you
you are crazy.
You can add your voice
all night to the voices
of a hundred and fifty others
in a circle
around a jailhouse
where your brothers and sisters are being held
for blocking buses with no lift,
or you can be one of the ones
inside the jailhouse,
knowing of the circle outside.
You can speak your love
to a friend
without fear.
You can find someone
who will listen to you
without judging you or doubting you or being
afraid of you

and let you hear yourself perhaps
for the first time.
These are all ways
of getting proud.
None of them
are easy, but all of them
are possible. You can do all of these things,
or just one of them again and again.
You get proud
by practicing.

Power makes you proud, and power
comes in many fine forms
supple and rich as butterfly wings.
It is music
when you practice opening your mouth
and liking what you hear
because it is the sound of your own
true voice.
It is sunlight
when you practice seeing
strength and beauty in everyone
including yourself.
It is dance
when you practice knowing
that what you do
and the way you do it
is the right way for you
and can't be called wrong.
All these hold

more power than weapons or money
or lies.
All these practices bring power, and power
makes you proud.
You get proud
by practicing.

Remember, you weren't the one
who made you ashamed,
but you are the one
who can make you proud.
Just practice,
practice until you get proud, and once you are proud,
keep practicing so you won't forget.
You get proud
by practicing.

Honor

Do I present
too great a challenge
to your ability to honor
another
as your equal?

I know what it is like for you, my
enlightened sisters.
I can sympathize now;
this conference has taught me
the pain,

for example: listening to labored language
english on a foreign tongue
the relief: to hear an american voice—strong, clear
and like mine
like mine.

How much more foreign we must seem, my
disabled sisters
and I.

When you talk of us at all,
you call us "the physically challenged,"
but I think the challenge
is yours.
For your vow to honor
all, equally
could mean

one woman might need you to carry a lunch plate and
    drink
across bumpy grass;
one might expect you to listen, listen to what she is
    saying,
listen, and ask "what?" when you don't understand;
another may want to serve on your committee,
make you look for a meeting place
without steps;
or a woman might need a push
or ask you to help empty her catheter bag

or fall in love with you

you might have to move my hand for me when it falls
away from my wheelchair's control
you might have to

touch me
touch me

honor me?
touch me.
honor me:
touch me

touch me

to be "physically challenged," means
more than being challenged
it means
being physical—

Is that what you want to share?

Translating the Crip

Can I translate myself to you?
Do I need to?
Do I want to?

When I say *crip* I mean flesh-proof power, flash mob
sticks and wheels in busy intersections, model
mock.

When I say *disability* I mean all the brilliant ways we
get through the planned fractures of the world.

When I say *living in America today* I mean thriving
and unwelcome, the irony of the only possible time
and place.

When I say *cure* I mean erase. I mean eradicate the
miracle of error.

When I say *safe* I mean no pill, no certified agency,
no danger to myself court order, no supervisory
setting, no nurse, can protect or defend or save me,
if you deny me power.

When I say *public transportation* I mean we all pay, we
all ride, we all wait. As long as necessary.

When I say *basic rights* I mean difficult curries, a
fancy-knotted scarf, a vegetable garden. I mean
picking up a friend at the airport. I mean two

blocks or a continent with switches or sensors or lightweight titanium, well-maintained and fully-funded. I mean shut up about charity, the GNP, pulling my own weight, and measuring my carbon footprint. I mean only embrace guaranteed can deliver real equality.

When I say *high-quality personal assistance services* I mean her sure hands earning honorably, and me eating and shitting without anyone's permission.

When I say *nondisabled* I mean all your precious tricks.

When I say *nondisabled privilege* I mean members-only thought processes, and the violence of stairs.

By *dancing* I mean of course dancing. We dance without coordination or hearing, because music wells through walls. You're invited, but don't do us any favors.

When I say *sexy* I mean our beautiful crip bodies, broken or bent, and whole. I mean drooling from habit and lust. I mean slow, slow.

When I say *family* I mean *all* the ways we need each other, beyond your hardening itch and paternal property rights, our encumbering love and ripping losses. I mean everything ripples.

When I say *normal* I don't really mean anything.

When I say *sunset, rich cheese, promise, breeze,* or *iambic pentameter,* I mean exactly the same things you mean.

Or, when I say *sunset* I mean swirling orange nightmare. When I say *rich cheese* I mean the best food I can still eat, or else I mean poverty and cholesterol. When I say *promise* I mean my survival depends on crossed digits. When I say *breeze* I mean finally requited desire. When I say *iambic pentameter,* I mean my heart's own nameless rhythm.

When I say *tell the truth* I mean complicate. Cry when it's no longer funny.

When I say *crip solidarity* I mean the grad school exam and the invisible man. I mean signed executive meetings, fighting for every SSI cent.

When I say *challenges to crip solidarity* I mean the colors missing from grant applications, the songs absent from laws. I mean that for all my complaints and victories, I am still sometimes more white than crip.

When I say anything I know the risk: You will accuse me of courage. I know your language all too well, steeped in its syntax of overcoming adversity and limited resources. When I say *courage* I mean you sitting next to me, talking, both of us refusing to compare or hate ourselves.

When I say *ally* I mean I'll get back to you. And you better be there.

Why I Am Not a Christian

I suppose it depends on what kind of solace
you are looking for.
For that must be what we seek
in the form of our prayers, and the messages returned
must be readable to us,
true answers.
And there are so many
willing messengers, we may
choose the voice, the dress code, the music,
the version of chapter and verse.
We may attend services at our convenience
among congregations characterized
by any combination of
political persuasion, age range, social class,
or sexual preference.
We may even choose
the message itself, how it soothes—
with encouragement, reason,
fear, or fellowship.

But always there is this wounded man
hanging above
watching blurrily through his blood.

Sometimes I go out into a cold wind
to feel it touching me
when no one else will.

What Kind of Death

How far away
to a secret   fertilized in fear?
How distant
the sterile lab
that sends back an answer   negative or
positive?

I knew him
as a friend   He told me his fear   the cough
perhaps more than just
what's going around

Reluctantly he sought
a test   an answer he hoped against

He told me his sadness   seeing
the waiting room crowded
with sick men   his brothers he called them
their youth destroyed
their love inhibited

He told me later   his relief
passing the test
false alarm
it wasn't in him   the cruel virus

Except
a year later he died

Why
the lie?
I was not just
his friend
I was his boss
he would have feared
for his job
He must have feared
to tell me
to tell anyone

for no one knew

What kind of death
must be so guarded?
What kind of death
must bring such shame?

Sex

We do it all the time.
We do it so many ways.
We keep them all wondering:
What do we do? they wonder.
Straight people wonder what lesbians do.
Lesbians wonder
what disabled lesbians do.
They all wonder.

They tease us,
threaten to videotape us at night,
but they never guess,
not even when it's right
in front of their eyes.

Sometimes it's not at night.
Sometimes, a whole week on the road
without a room to ourselves,
we can't do anything at night.
But we do it so many ways.

Fingers. Raisins. Mouths.
Soft strong fingers, tender raisins,
open mouth.
It's easier than stopping for lunch
on the long miles between cities,
filling our stomachs and our bloodstreams
with raisins.
Your five strong fingers

organize themselves around raisins,
clumps of two or three,
push them easily into my waiting mouth.
I chew,
swallow,
taste the sugar,
then open again for more.

We do it all the time, so many ways,
raisins in the car or

warm nuggets that must be water,
sweeter than raisins,
your fingers push into me,
pellets of water that open,
water I feel pouring down the
insides of my legs,
water that changes to fire
and stays water
water that bursts
from the bottoms of my burning
feet.

Sending a Message

Whatever there is
that can be prayed to:
Hear me.

Yesterday I sent my friend
a poem.
Both her color eyes, and mine,
were in it.
Her name was in it, her robin-spirit.
And my lingering affection.

As she reads it, give her
a clear light.

Carry our brief, shared memories
into a glass globe. Hold it to her,
let her peer in.
Show her a future flowering.
Bless us with magic, and bring it true.

Bring it true.
Oh bring it true.

Rain Traffic

On wet streets, tires sound
like pulling the skin
off a ripe orange.

Progress

At last, I thought,
we are making some progress;
at least, I thought,
we're talking about it now.

She brought it up, saying
she was interested,
romantically—she wanted me
to know. But

then she said
she wouldn't know what to do
with me
in a wheelchair, and hardly
able to move.

So I wrote her a poem, offering
a few suggestions,
and informing her of the
relevant facts: That my skin
was ready to dance   my skin and hers
could enjoy all kinds
of choreography swing to our souls' orchestrations
That my thighs were alive, afire
between them melting
a swirling core
That my mouth
ached for her water
one bright drop   let's mix our surfs

over a new island, our island
Why not
when all our senses work fine
only waiting to join hot
and wrestle in a whirlpool   waltzing
Grab hold, said the poem for me

Then she said
that in relationships she was never
the aggressor.

So I wrote a poem
that when read a certain way
took charge   took her   laid her
down turned her over and held us bound
together up and down:
nose to cheek to cheek to nose
chin against neck   belly by belly
legs locked
exposed centers pressed
together, wriggling
like movie hostages
and then let
our tiniest involuntary reactions
take over from here: synapses exploding
like popcorn   sharp   tender
forcing hot quick   our breaths
carrying us
to sudden darkness

Then she said
that she feared having me grow
to depend on her.

So I wrote a poem
disavowing any such need   except
as suited the moment
which might be brief
and unique
as a web of saliva left spun
by our tongues
No need,   said the poem for me,
to be careful   I can stand to hurt
I'll grow again from a new place

Now she says
she doesn't know.

Someday I'll ask her
no paper between us
Girl, when you gonna get your shit together
so we can have this fling?

On the Lawn

We met on the lawn the first day.

We met on the lawn, ready for talk,
not knowing how soon, how urgently, our talk would
    begin.

We met on the lawn, half-unbelieving,
with the sun on our skins,
the sound of jackhammers in our ears.

We met on the lawn,
red with anger
and the African morning heat,
leaving a cool room empty.

We met on the lawn
the first day of the conference
and every other day after that
among the world's women,
and in growing numbers,

we met on the lawn.
The program's schedule had read,
"Problems of Handicapped Women."
Perhaps it was thought that none would attend:
The lift in the program's scheduled building
was broken.

We met on the university lawn,
finding each other easily among the world's women.
We formed a group, forty strong, distinguishable by
    canes,
wheelchairs, signed language,
and a large white-blue banner—
familiar woman symbol, circle atop a cross
with the circle broken.

We met on the lawn because the lift
wasn't working.
The combined resources of the University of Nairobi,
the United Nations,
and President Daniel Arap Moi
had not been mobilized
to fix it.
We demanded to be heard.

We met on the lawn the second day
with Dame Nita Barrow of Barbados, convener from
    the U.N.
Yes, the lift would be fixed. Yes, volunteer girl scouts
to assist as needed. Yes, an information table.
Her deep, elegant voice indicated
she owned this conference
and would be pleased to share it all round.
She gave us smiles, and yes, yes, yes.
We never saw the girl scouts.

We met on the lawn in front of the building,
choosing our space because
we had no choice but to choose.
Inside,
the world's women spoke to each other across barriers
of tongue and mind.
Outside,
eighteen steps led
to the building's front door.
So even on the third day, when the lift was fixed,

we met on the lawn.
But we had come this far, and we too wanted to share
and be with the world's women.
We would, though it meant a sightless climb
or upward bumping
in the hands of men and strangers.
We would fold paper birds with Japanese women for
    peace,
learn ancient female rites,
hear a Palestinian woman ask
where, where to build an abortion clinic.
But when we met with each other,

we met on the lawn.
We were all the world's women
African, European, North American, Asian,
    Australian.
When we first came together I wondered

that so many of us would have ourselves conveyed
    here,
wriggling, stretching, being hoisted into
    uncomfortable,
impoverished modes of coming and going—airplanes,
    taxis,
the hands of men and strangers.
We all come from communities of struggling,
    strengthened women.
Compared with our sisters,
we are rich; we are here.
But it's our poverty that draws us together.

We met on the lawn;
university buildings surrounded us,
and more women than I imagine would ever gather.

One of the times I made it to the third-floor window,
I looked down
on all the world's women,
laid before me like a shifting map—
and our group among them, adding to the group's
    strength.
Colors of clothing appeared as flags—
each could have been in her own country.

We met on the lawn under our own flag:
blue-on-white woman symbol,
circle broken open.

Four days would teach me that break was no flaw.
I was quest, discovery, embrace.
From our torn, strong lives
we patched a statement, writing the truth we knew.
Painstakingly our words stitched a protest,
shaped an open circle of stores,
always room for more.

We met on the lawn in a ragged, broken circle
under our broken-circle banner of female welcoming.
Our periphery unfolded,
like a pink, cabbage-sized African flower,
like the eight long days of the conference,
and invited in others
of the world's women.
A woman from Iran, dark-agate-eyes and earnest,
watched us silently for days where

we met on the lawn.
She approached finally, asking to join in writing our
    statement.
Her leg was gone below the knee.
She wanted us to condemn war, that disables.
We agreed.
Then she wanted us to condemn Iraq,
that disabled her.
When we refused, she left us.

We met on the lawn under the weight of Africa's sun
and our own contradictions.
We were among,
and apart from,
the world's women,
adding, as if to a flag, the colors of knowledge,
    of feeling,
we determined they should see. We wove and waved
    it as

we met on the lawn.
Out of nowhere?
Is that what the world's women would think?
But it was not out of nowhere.
We had been there all along.
We have been here all along.

We met on the lawn on hot afternoons
using what languages we knew.
Linda, Louise, Stella and I found common ground
    in French,
used it to measure our lives' shape in an African city,
a Canadian province, the U.S., and here, where

we met on the lawn.
Everywhere we found sharp edges cut
on statistically inevitable occurrences
of physical disability.

We met on the lawn, last day,
telling a few reporters about access, understanding,
    language,
and the clean-up of Nairobi's streets.

We met on the African lawn while disabled Africans
began their slow scramble back from the
    impoverished suburbs.

We met on the lawn
not knowing the impact on ourselves or the world.
we will not know for many years.

We met on the lawn in July 1985.

We met on the lawn.

Petrona

I forgot to ask her
how she got to their doors.

"The men said
that because we weren't veterans,
we didn't have the right
to participate
in the organization."

I wondered whether
she ever challenged their definitions,
ever compared her veteran status
to theirs.
Didn't she survive
the same Somoza as they?
Didn't she live to see
the same hopeful revolution?
Didn't Contra attacks replace her safety
with the same insecurity and fear?
And didn't she endure
another battle as well?—Petrona, veteran
of the birth of her own child,
wounded by medicine, the hands of healers.
She reaped her disability
as unwillingly, as valiantly as any soldier.
She did not deserve
their rejection.

"It was for that reason
that I began to organize
disabled women.
I would visit them
house by house
until we formed a group."

Astonished, I admired
her casualness, mentioning
what this organization became—
one hundred eighty
active members;
one hundred eighty
activist disabled women.
In my rich country, I'm lucky
sometimes to gather
half a dozen disabled women.
How did she do it?

"The same necessity
to organize
makes you have to learn.
You learn
as you go along
to formulate strategies for your own survival
and for the survival of the organization.
It's a hard road,
but at the end
you obtain tenacity."

I pictured her
navigating that hard road—
broken sidewalks, unramped corners,
rutted streets.
Perhaps she took her children with her;
perhaps they pushed and tugged on her chair
when a wheel caught in a crack.
What did she say
as she approached the homes, the families—
first her neighbors,
and then beyond?
Did she ask them, "*Who else is inside?*"
Did she say, "*I would like to meet
your daughter, whom you haven't sent to school.*"
Did she say, "*Let me talk
to your wife, who does not come to the market anymore.*"
Did she say, "*Please give this flyer
about our meeting
to your sister; and tell her
I will visit again soon.*"

Petrona didn't tell me all this.
She only said,
"I would visit them
house by house
until we formed a group."

I forgot to ask her
about narrow gates into yards,
about steps onto porches.

I forgot to ask her
how she got to their doors.

Petunias

I knew you planned
—you knew I supported—
this arrest.

Yet when I watched you,
unstoppable as ever,
driving your chair
around a cop,
up a hill,
through careful, distinctly unrevolutionary
petunias,
past a police barricade,
and knew I'd probably seen
the last for at least
that day
of you—
my selfish spirit whispered
a small wish
to call you back,
forget the cause,
abandon the movement,
pick some petunias,
and take you home.

Another whisper reminded me
how fragile
our home might be.
The world we share
—our meals, our bed,

our work, our freedom to live
together
alone—
depends on this clash
and on our mutual
—you of your liberty
one or two days
—me of you
in my bed—
sacrifice.

I wanted right then
to offer—like a hand-picked bouquet—
my small insight
to you, and hear
your thoughts in turn.

But by then I could see
no sign of you
except
your tire marks through the petunias.

etc.

she speaks
strong convincing speech
of women
of black women but also
of all women
almost all women
black women   etc.   i am the etc.

she celebrates women

   black women women of color white women etc.
                                                 i am the etc.
   working class women middle class women privileged
      women
   homeless women poor and destitute women etc.
                                                 i am the etc.
   lesbian bisexual straight single ex- etc.
                                                 i am the etc.
   mother grandmother sister friend etc.
                                                 i am the etc.

she names the actions of women
   powerful radical reformist etc.
                                            we are the etc.
she distinguishes women and men
   oppressors allies leaders etc.
                                            we are the etc.
                                               .

   she doesn't do this to divide people
   people are divided already

she does this to analyze
to challenge

                beside me among these hundred
                        you turn now and then
                        with a nod or a whispered comment
                                we both agree
                        with most of what she says
but   we both know
                        whom she leaves out

                                you too are the etc.
she identifies differences

gender   race class nationality sexual practice etc.

                                        i am the etc.

bell hooks
fierce feminist brilliant writer   woman not afraid
to dig for the root
     etc. doesn't do her potent ideas justice
     her critiques fit me
     her visions fit me
     but   i don't fit her words
     except etc.

                                (i do like that term:
          sexual practice)

in practice

sexuality seethes with meaning   possibility
   connection
intimacy   desire   revolution   etc.
              that's an etc. i can dig
                   to the root
                   beside me
                   your new haircut
            haloes the shape of your ear
                   i think about
                   kissing you

                        etc.

Fertility Goddess—*a Sestina*

Her five-dollar yardsale price tag does nothing
(we hope) to diminish the quiet power
residing in her beads and cowrie shells, in her smooth
    round shape.
We bring her home, dust her a little; we stand
her on a molding over the dining room door
to the extra bedroom. She is real, in the sense of real
    wood.

The realness of her divinity remains
to be seen; but there's almost nothing
we won't try, now, to get through that door
guarded by the Department of Social Services' powers
that be. Sternly, rulebook in hand, they stand
admitting or denying entrance. Judging by the shape

of us, by our wheelchairs, they decide we are in no
    shape
to supervise young children. How on earth could
we rescue them from fires, from soiled beds? One
    of us cannot stand;
the other barely walks. We are outraged: Knowing
    nothing
about us, how dare they use their power
to shut, to lock, this door?

We appeal. Under hinted threat of suit, they send
a social worker to our door.
Cheerfully, she fills out forms; inspects the size and
    shape

of the extra bedroom. She compliments our hardwood
floors; our educational achievements; the generous
    power
of our desire. "God wants you to have a child,"
she says. (To this we say nothing.
We will smile, for now; play their games; and prepare
    to take a stand

when we must.) During the interview, our fertility
    goddess stands
watching, listening, from her perch above the door.
Unlike the social worker's God, our goddess wants
    nothing, directs nothing.
She doesn't work that way.
Instead, she waits, carrying the weight and shape
of what we want. All our hope and doubt gestates
in the dense wood of her body. With the power

she brought along, pent-up and palpable, she
    nourishes the force
of our dreams. For years she waited, displayed on an
    old man's shelf
or bookstand, never called upon, never impregnated; a
    mere artifact.
Finally, one hot Saturday, we carried her through our
    door
to play a part in the drama just starting to take shape
in our lives, which might lead to nothing—

our hearts broken, our power wasted by a system
that would rather bar its door to us than find a child
    a home—
or might, after all, let us shape
and cherish a child, teach her to stand proud
and let the world deny her nothing.

Pain Too

I dream
of pain too
not the always ache
of emptiness
but full pain new pain
that will go away
pain holding tight
my hands
and
pain to wet my face
gasping
against the loss
of happiness
I dream
the birth of pain
fathered by happiness
I dream
of pain nurtured
in happiness
I dream
yes
I dream
of happiness
and
I dream
of pain too

Praise

So much to praise
even the silvery green of antifreeze
glowing on black asphalt   is beautiful   It forms
like a puddle   but grows
like a snake
gaining   not losing   momentum as it goes
I stare, angry at having
this much time   to kill
awaiting a late bus   but still
it is beautiful

I will remember it   weeks away   miles later
among aspen and lodgepole pine   where wind
and fragments of sun   pull cool water
from my quenched skin
In the forest I will praise
the unloved city   which birthed
the snake

Oral History Project:
Interviewing My Mother

She stopped, just like that, 1960,
a Republican singles' mixer where she met "the one."
They would marry, become lifelong Democrats,
monthly bridge players, martini drinkers,
my parents,
with burdens and conflicts I want to hear.
But she stopped, not telling me we were done, just
never came for an eighth session. The stories end with
her fingers speed-typing oil production reports,
background clack of jackhammer adding
new steel and glass office towers around
her Petroleum Club Building,
southern suburban foothills growing
ranch homes on acre lots
that would soon house families like ours
with male breadwinners and blonde kids.
In the stories, she still wore smart dresses and pearls,
ran adding machines, fancy new printers, office pools;
still chatted and laughed with the other secretaries
and the men they worked for, got the coffee gladly.
She dated geologists, engineers, businessmen,
shared apartments with the other girls.
She skied at Winter Park, slept at Ed's Beds.
She'd started as I'd asked, 1934,
Pomeroy, Ohio,
second daughter
of Arthur Howard Roush, trainmaster, and
Velma Lucille French Roush, homemaker.

She pushed out almost three decades' details:
tiny schools, anxious mother, harsh father, scarlet fever,
friends who rarely visited, school prize, baby brother,
    leaving
for college, running out of savings.
She lingered over that one year at Ohio State,
the best year of her life.

No Deal

*Dedicated to those who voted for Colorado's
Amendment #2, legalizing discrimination against
lesbians and gays.*

If you are asking me
to trade my family—
        warm dream ocean nights
        mornings reluctant
        days reckless balance of survival and vision
        laughing women evenings—
for yours—
Forget it.

If you are asking me
to swap my values—
        respect for people irreverence for prestige
        yearning honoring great mother spirit
        fear of poison love of peace
        insistence on autonomy
        welcome responsibility
for yours—
No deal.

If I must give up
what I know of passion—
        flamewater torrents occurring
        in circles cast by glowpaper moon
        steady sentences hanging mistletoe year-round
        and sweet punctuation exercises—

in favor of
a safe hand in hand stroll with an approved lover—
Huh-uh.

If you want
my woman-self originality
in exchange for your stern conformity
as the price for my equality—
I'm sorry.
If you demand
contrition as a necessary condition
for acceptance
then—
Thanks but no thanks.

This is no deal you're offering—
this is erasure.
> But the words keep coming back.
> I go on writing my way.
> I go on making my love.
> I go on refusing your shame.
> I go on deciding on pride.
> I go on cherishing my friends.
> I go on speaking my fear.
> I go on finding my strength.
> I go on living my life.

And you've got
no deal.

Morning Contact

your voice breaking over the phone
broke against my morning
bumped against   almost broke
my heart
or something near it

already i had heard   checking from pay phones
three days of messages
recording your efforted speech
as we tried to
make our daily   distant contact

i explained   though you know
how busy i've been
both of us so busy

now
your testimony of loneliness
weighed on me
you told me to ignore   everything
you might say   today   you need to be down

i hate   you said   being in love

i was afraid this might happen
i am guilty of your pain
a sweet burden i never
thought i'd earn

my own pain i mostly
allowed to harden in place   until time or busy-
ness   eventually   scraped it off

yours is different
it thickens and flows between us
as richly
as our wanting

Loyalty

The poet in me wants
to be out there, beyond the pane
with the other poets.
The poet in me wants
to meet and greet,
get my gay on,
shine my wit, my stories:
>march of buoyant wheeling protests around
>marble departments;
>songs on long bumpy bus rides from Beijing
>to muddy Huairou.

Can the poet forgo a rich exchange of tales
under August stars, stay instead
beside the tired body
just breathing in this darkened room?

It's so tempting.
Imagine friendship incubated in deep reserves
of stamina and eloquent gesture.
Imagine so much lung capacity
you can afford to burn some of it away
in loud laughter and tobacco leaf.
Imagine writing about reliable bodies
striding unpaved rocky terrain,
and coupling toward revolution.

Can the poet in me attend
this aching body?

Can I love *this* poetry—
this whisper of sore lungs
        that reach to seduce coy air;
this enjambment,
        when each gurgle does the work of lost
        muscle;
this rhythm of heartbeat
        shallowly telling urgent secrets;
this syntax of tongue
        sandstone dry but remembering sweet;
this howl of a throbbing head,
        humming warehouse of crumbling
        manuscripts;
this curving rhyme scheme of spine
        stressed, but at rest;
this groan of grateful skin
        grown quiet at the margins;
this background noise of premenstrual sweat;
this free verse of twisted hips;
this metaphor of hoarse voice?

Like Air

Like air
we float kite words
fragile signals
and hearts flap
purple wings

Like air
my struggling lungs
seize you
gasp relief
release long-held breaths
desire
expanding
capacity unknown
welcoming gulps
of future

Like air
I need clarity
shot through with sunlight
invisibly to buoy me
towards an idea called
us
My dreams
are mostly silent
Does something
besides distance
obscure us?

Like air
intimacy should be a right
for now
it is only a promise

Like air
you travel my blood's hungry stream
to every limb
this is how
for now
we touch

Labors of Love

Everything.
Everything.
Everything.
Everything.

Do everything. Do everything.

Can't do
everything.
Can't
do everything.

Can't
do everything can't
do

everything.

I can't do everything, you say.

What should I ask
of you then?
Everything
I need:
a drink a bite a call
a touch to place me somewhere on Earth
labors of love

laughter
lightness of touch
intensity of passion
a ride to my meeting

tortillas and apple juice
on sale
a touch
of reassurance curiosity or absent-minded connection
cash until Friday

and patience desire energy and love
undying

Intermission

The standoff with police
lulls like an intermission—
tension plateaus
our chanting dims—
hot concrete ground is claimed   or boundaried
wheelchair tire against boot
muscles against brake
they keep us waiting
rented buses with lifts   and drivers on overtime
on their way
to take away those who will still
not move—

Nervous young cops
watch us closely
wordlessly
wonder what they're supposed to do with us
listen anxiously for a radioed word
when will the buses arrive

Meanwhile   sometimes
while we wait
we talk
to each other

Eric is careful
keeping his cigarette away from my oxygen tank
his keen eyes follow my lips' motions
my words' shapes—

with no movement to my hands
I can't speak his language—
but he speaks mine
remembering what sound sounds like

Smiling
he talks of what he's lost—
hearing   strength in his legs   most of his
    stamina
a career in medicine

Smiling
squinting against the sun
he talks of what he's gained—
this battle   these friends
how he's grown—
from a doctor's arrogance   to the vulnerability
    of a patient
a better person
a gentle fighter

He concludes—no shred of irony—calling his
    disability
the best thing that ever happened
to him

In fact not until later would any   irony
occur to me
not until the week was over

the demonstrations done
the protestors disbursed

For now I was still accustomed
to the rhythm of chanting
and the knack for observing our histories
without shame—
I had grown used
to casual exchanges of pride
under the wary stares of police

Drink

I think of you thirstily. My mouth
swells a little with ache
to take the shapes that pour forth
from you, salted by an atmosphere
I thought I'd never taste.
Our clicking tongues
sought and found   sought and found
draw from each other
springs
never again to hide.
How we bathed in the discovery!

I think of you thirstily, listen
to the tumbling play
of your voice, faraway music
of brook over rocks.
You are my dream,
a new-found source of sustenance
existing simultaneously
in you
and me.

I think of you thirstily. You have
lakes I want to drain
and fill   drain and fill.
Gulping from you,
I am a greedy bird
wanting water.

I think of you thirstily. Even from there,
you, faraway brook music, you
shower me,
and open invitation to open wide.
and like a dazed turkey
I gaze up,   up,
not caring if I drown.

Don't Hold Hands While They Feed You

"Don't bite the hand that feeds you"
is a standard American rule;
it urges obedience, and paying your dues
to the owners and providers of gruel.

There's a restaurant here in Denver
with a warning at the gate,
asking customers to remember
conduct proper—that is, straight!

If two women are dining together,
or likewise a man and a man,
if two walk in as birds of a feather,
they must never, ever hold hands!

Don't hold hands while they feed you,
especially if you're gay,
or if the manager sees you,
you'll be scolded and sent on your way.

The owners of the White Spot
will defend their pure, good name
from the scandalous, fearful blot
of hand-holding by genders the same.

Some might try to remind us
that this is the land of the free,
and that holding hands is harmless,
whoever the couple may be.

But White Spot paid good money
to build upon this plot;
so when you go in, and pay your money,
White Spot calls the shots.

Money talks, that's a fact,
that's what it's all about.
But if they can tell gays how to act,
harass us, throw us out,

then how much longer will it be
before the watchful eye
falls on you as well as me
and it's too late to wonder why.

Ill at Ease

A sickness goes around
goes with the ticking of the clock
goes with the massing of the troops
goes with the arguments around the dinner table
goes with the growing threat of war.
My mother had it last Thursday,
nauseous all night,
blaming the seafood,
admitting later it was her anger,
so upset was she about
the ease with which our country goes
to war.
A man I saw on television
had the same bug.
He told the camera he has been physically sick,
that's why he marches
in the streets of Washington, D.C.
These are people for whom
the war is not easy.
They cannot easily
eat their dinner
watch their TV
drive their cars
pay their taxes
while body bags are shipped out in
return.
They cannot digest
the news.

They cannot digest
the reasons.
They cannot digest
the lies.

May the contagion spread, may indigestion
upset the feast,
the stomach that gorges
on cheap oil,
blood,
and belief in a false history, a history
in which American has the right
is the right
a history in which there is no history
leading to this false inevitability
a history which is ignored until
there is no option
except that which should never be an option.
May the sickness
touch us all, lest we ever,
as long as this war lasts,
be at ease.

Hunger

all that holds me i hunger
wordless
from the inside
it cradles my yawning heart,
carries my dark brain in its
strong grasp, smooths my hair, rocks
the furious fists with which i solicit
a breast

hunger has large arms   but no breasts
it is like a man: wordless, strange
all hard bones and muscles
or a shell-dwelling clam
it can dig a bed but i cannot
sing

while sometimes i wait
thinking someone is about to happen
hunger starts throwing
gaps of ground out from under me
my tunnel caves in

hunger has a rusty shovel   but no cunt
it builds a crumbling dam to sop
my river but no
river to join it

yes i mean i am hungry
hungry for the breast

hungry for the song
hungry for the earth
hungry for the cunt
i am hungry

i am hungry
hunger holds me
and chews on my thighs
when i roll to hunger's caresses
then
i am not a woman—
i am food

Hands

They poke knowledgeably
tender swollen tissue,
efficiently they stretch the contracted limb
until pain answers a question.
His hands have become owners
of a skill,
have acquired the power
to name disease
like the power a machine has
to stamp, to label, to seal,
its aiming arm a hammer
of precision.

His hands
act upon me a drama of question
and answer, a loveless logic.
His hands
etch solutions
to the incomplete equations of my body,
or pronounce them
insoluble.
His hands
inspire me to nightmare silence
as I offer up to him,
like sacrifices to his godhood,
the damaged
hurting flesh.

Rage worms
into the earth of my throat, buries itself
lest it thwart the search for what's needed,
the coveted cure.
They must not be offended, those hands,
those prized instruments,
those weapons
of healing.

The Ones Who Go to Jail

The ones who go to jail
are the ones
who remember and describe each city
not by its sights, its restaurants, its rivers—
but by its capacity
and mechanisms
for justice.
They remembering the gentleness or anger of police
    —whose claims to be
    "only doing a job"
    go just as far as their willingness
    to commit, or diffuse, violence;
    to cause, or relieve, pain;
    and not one inch further.
They remember the cell
or the gymnasium, hastily furnished with cots
to accommodate
dozens of women and men,
dozens of wheelchairs,
and physical needs
which are mundane to us,
but unheard-of
to the frightened guards assigned to meet them:
    —cumedin, laoricil, lasix;
    battery chargers, ventilator masks,
    egg-crate mattresses;
    emptying a leg-bag full of urine,
    helping heavy, stiff bodies onto low cots—

and as the ones who go to jail
insist on their right
to assistance in the bathroom;
as they demand to fed,
bite by bite;
they know they echo the call of our people.
Their hearts and their actions
harmonize the call:
> Where once there was shame,
> let us cultivate pride!
> Where we have needs,
> let us be dependent no more!
> Where we ask for assistance
> let it be a right!
> Where institutions have monopolized
> the lives of our people,
> now let their doors close,
> let their owners be bankrupt!

The ones who go to jail
both choose
and do not choose
their confinement.

They may wear each arrest
gaudily, like a feather, like the bumper stickers
on their wheelchairs;
trade stories; add up days served.
They may anticipate the next arrest
with enthusiasm and bravado.

They may, like Eileen, who calls herself Spitfire,
present an open-armed invitation
to be the first one taken.
They may watch, level-eyed, the police,
until they know their warnings
are finally serious—
and remain, nevertheless, at their chosen post,
locking their brakes,
blocking their doors.

Yet the ones who go to jail
would not choose this—
not if they could learn to forget
the ones who have no choice,
the ones confined
in a different kind of prison.
The ones who go to jail
cannot forget.
They think of the sisters and brothers,
think of the old and the young,
think of our own pasts, of our own impounded futures.
The ones who go to jail
think about the ones
who go to nursing homes—
and choose gladly.

Ghost

under the warming sheet
an arm
another arm
reaching
then gone

eyes close deliberately
without comfort

something lifts
a cool breeze under
the sheet
but
only the only body i know
is there

a ghost
who never lived
haunts
my dreamless nights

circles without touch
plays
inconclusively in the dark

wisp-straws travel
along legs and neck
breath deepens

still
only the only body i love
is there

Flights

Stairs have ceased to be poetic.
A tight doorway, a curb, a broken elevator,
the lack of a ramp—
for me, these hurdles quicken no creativity,
no bursts of verse.
Flights of stairs no longer launch
flights of my imagination.

Ten years ago these obstructions
awakened our voices,
drew us forward into battle,
forged our unity.
In Nairobi we gathered, one by one,
from our villages, cities, homes, farms, schools, nations.
Women with disabilities, separated from our sisters
by walls and risers, found our own sisterhood.

Barriers pushed us into margins where we met:
outside the meeting rooms,
at the foot of the stairs,
on the lawn.

Denied our rightful place,
we transformed the obstacles
into a concrete image of our oppression;
a border linking our lives;
a symbol of our connection;
a stage for our angry words.

We gathered to protest our exclusion,
found we had much more to share; our nuanced lives
as workers, as mothers, as daughters, as fighters—
But that was ten years ago.

Stairs are no longer poetic.
Barriers drain strength from our arms and hearts,
animate neither verse no dance.
We are tired of the fight.
Banishment still sets our anger in motion
but no longer makes us sing.

Fingers

Another loss, a decade ago, so recent:
a fine motor skill, once had,
still recalled.

Shadows in my dreams
cut out all that is unnecessary.
Only the central figures exist,

including myself, and stay
in one corner of the dark, night-hushed
café. My arms rest

across a white surface, smooth and cool,
a clean board usually announcing
daily specials. In remembered motion, my fingers

curl around a thick blue pen
a loose grasp. Slowly I form
block letters, ugly but useful.

When asked,
I always deny dreaming
about walking

and am offended when others dream it for me—
as if I would be better that way,
as if I should be more like the dreamer.

When I am the dreamer,
I find my chair carries me, as well as in daylight,
wherever the dream may lead:

to joyous fiery carnivals, erupting yellow and red;
to a secret garage, a friend who won't be ignored;
to a dark, night-hushed café.

Every time, it's I, the dreamer—
in my body, in my wheelchair—
dreaming myself as I am.

Only tonight, my fingers are remembering
something lost.
Tonight,

I'm drawing letters
with
my own hand.

Which letters, I don't remember;
nor their meaning,
nor their message. I only

remember the motion,
remember the aim, remember
the remembering.

Eating

teeth cage the invited culprit
before the offense
tongue gentle teasing while incisors caress
mold right shapes
to swallow
careful not too
large
loose
or thick
no sharp   cracker corners   broccoli florets
     salmon bones
these are the things
I know

and ice
a bite or two   every few bites
and when
the way   becomes blocked

natural life-giving greed
becomes my hazard
I fight   lovingly   for the pleasure   but fear forgets

fear hears only
words
of doctors who only
talk of danger
talk of weakness
talk of the unexpected
future

fear forgets   the unexpected power
of my own
self-amplifying
voice
fear forgets

fear sees only
the ghost-white video x-ray
the chalky white liquid
stuck
in the mapped white pockets
of my throat
fear forgets fire
orange red leaping
fear forgets the blue healing
flakes falling
through me
fear forgets

fear understands
the problem
but fear forgets   me
fear forgets me

dusk

moving through the stillness at dusk
my breathing draws in
some of that quiet—

carries it like something fragile—
a snowflake or a grasshopper—
hurt but still breathing

as if
    brought home   laid out on cleared tablespace
it could be examined

nursed
helped to grow

delicate fold of moon
single diamond piercing its soft lobe—
       the sky cocks an ear
       to listen

Development

You
were once only an idea
to me.
We met.
I carried you with me
like a theory I could not
test, a conjecture never
to be confirmed.
So it must have been
an unscientific trust that kept you there,
my thoughts abounding
with your smile, your laugh,
your penetrating, sky-hued eyes.
It was a faith I couldn't
believe in, rehearsed
without conviction.
But somehow,
you came true, true
as the line crossing
a steep perilous sun-frosted
hill you ski
without fear.
How we are real
as a rainbow, captured
on film
or not.

Dawn-Pull

Our eyelids press
unsuccessfully against the masked

cold sun   We roll,
wishing comfort could last

Reluctance urges me awake   The dawn
will pull our bodies apart

for another day   Only
your nearness can keep me warm

on cold mornings   We try
our voices, telling

our dreams
without mentioning they are dreams

"I learned to fly a magic carpet"
"We were adopting a baby   We waited

in the hospital to see her"
You smile at that

The Cops vs. ADAPT

Baltimore, Maryland, April 30, 1991
Demonstrations and civil disobedience carried out by
American Disabled for Attendant Programs Today, at
office of the Health Care Finance Authority, to protest
federal spending which favors nursing home placement
over independent living options for people with
disabilities.

straight steps

our steps could never
(those of us who can step)
our steps could never be so straight

timed marching

if we could march
our march would be fast
and slow
all falling in time
with what each needed

orders followed

we are an effusion
of angry energy
that
and the discovery
of pride
are what fuel us

crisp uniforms

                  the sleeves of our T-shirts tell
                the history of our movement
                           city to city
      some of us have worn the same blue jeans
                        for three days

restraint
discipline

                        we are laughter
                      fire unabashed
                      friendly riot
        the inconvenient truth in your face

intimidation the always-present threat
of force

                      we are unafraid
                      as we face off
              outnumbering by only
                      two to one

the well-trained well-armed forces
sent to control us
equipped with clubs
guns
helicopters

bodily strength
the power
to arrest
to imprison us
for our disobedience

we are unafraid
for too many of us have already
been imprisoned
too many sisters
too many brothers still
locked away
not for disobedience
but for disability
such simple needs
dressing
bathing
eating
simple needs which bring
a life sentence

in precise drill
they flaunt the power
others have to
rule their steps

our jagged line
cannot be ruled

stone jaws unmoving eyes

we are a medley
of spastic movements
pantomime
wandering eyes
open mouths
restlessness
pounding chant

our resolve is a song

theirs is a regimen

we sing protest against
the captivity of thousands
we shout against emptiness
those missing lives

under the glare
damp east coast sun
under the glare
a straight line of police

we plumb our bounds
we embrace our freedom

Connection

the way you acknowledge me
lover
makes me bloom
and then you extol my blooming

the way you acknowledge me
spirit
sent me in search of myself
i am still searching
will you join me in finding

the way you acknowledge me
friend
webs me to all the earth's creatures
strengthened strands of love

you gave me back my birthright
that i had forgotten

Big Clouds

Maybe I avoid dreaming
because wounds sustained in daytime
stay invisible
only to light.

At night I listen
as big clouds move into
a scalded sky.
Every time the planet turns
it pulls with it these damaged atmospherics.
Get political about it
or not—
it's a thing we live with,
will maybe die with.

Something similar
follows me in my turning. The grief I choose to swallow
sticks, and sometimes
comes up again, all around me,
waste that backs up and floating, cuts right through
my skin.
Like a movement, I throw my members
into the fight for a hospitable world:
Greenpeace to my own soul.

But pollution whispers
so inaudibly.

The sounds in my house are more commanding.
I tell myself, It's the furnace,
It's the wind.
I don't take these sounds seriously,
but they are sounds.
They conjure
real images, real possibilities, of armed intruders,
of scared boys.

I listen, and conjure, until the cold
bite of my own eardrum
lets go

and leaves me
wrapped in the torn bandages
of restive sleep

And She Will Also Want to Draw the Water

"They come with these development projects, come
to the villages," said the woman from Zimbabwe.
"And they work with the women there,
all the women there."
(She spoke deeply
holding the attention of women from everywhere
on the sunny University of Nairobi lawn. Though she
    was not,
like most of us,
disabled,
we listened raptly.)
"And never is thought given
to the disabled woman there. Never
is she considered."
(Heads in the group, of women intent,
were nodding.)
"And the disabled woman, she will be there.
And she will be raising a family, too.
They will put in the water projects,
the new water projects.
These are not very accessible at all,
not accessible to the disabled woman.
And she will also want to draw the water.
And they do not think about it at all."

Women from everywhere,
women with brightly-colored khangas wrapped
round their bodies and heads, women wearing
blue jeans and backpacks,
nodded again.

Women from everywhere,
women with disabilities,
understood.
Each thought about her life,
about the lives around her,
here, and back home:
disabled women's lives.
And each thought about killing
invisibility.

How much harder work is
      when nobody believes you work.
      Nobody believes you work.
How lonely is raising your children
      when no one thinks you have sex,
      no one thinks you can have sex.
How just being there can drain you
      when it feels as though you're not.
      You're not there. You're not there.
What struggles face the survivor
      who never should have survived.
We are all survivors;
we are all impossible women.

The truest translation of the day
came from the words of two women
from Tanzania. Both use crutches,
and came to this neighboring country

on a bus
with the English sister who runs their vocational school.
"When a disabled woman is born," the sister dubbed,
"it is thought
that she is not possible."
She quickly corrected herself, rendered again:
"It is thought
that she has no possibilities."

But the women from everywhere,
disabled women,
understood the syntax of both
sentences.
How can we have possibilities
while we ourselves
are not thought
possible?

Our very lives are a source,
for some,
of amazement
        "I don't know how you cope."
of wonder
        "A baby? You had a baby?"
of disbelief
        "What happened?"
And those are the few, the ones made half-aware

by chance.
For most, we are simply
not there.

> "When a disabled woman is born,
> it is thought
> that she is not possible."

We are all survivors;
we are all impossible women.

> "The disabled woman, she will be there
> and she will also want to draw the water."

Yes, we are there,
will go on being there.
We are here.

One King Bed, Non-Smoking, Conference Rate, Access

We knew we had between us three
skilled hands and tongues and hearts.
Two of us could hear; each could see

the words we lipped like ghee
with the code-cracking arts
we knew we had between us three.

You here, you there, between you me.
Honor our pauses and restarts.
Two of us could hear; each could see

and teach without etymology
words for waken, strum; the quaking parts
we opened up between us three.

We sucked and spilled our Snapple tea,
theorized what cripqueer imparts
of we who talk, fuck, hear and see

against norms and claim authority.
In sticky sheets we rose like tarts
to know again between us three
a burst of want we cried to hear and see.

Adventure

This to me is adventure:

crossing marginally Burnside the Willamette
a pair of wheelchairs
cars and river rushing perpendicular our path
sleet falling and night
cold eating
into the muscles I have left
sharp wind bringing
a recurrent tear to my healing eye
exasperated
with my lover half a block ahead
who couldn't wait for the bus
no
we had to do this on our own
our own wheels

as my good thumb stiffens
my sight comes alive
despite the cold
to the darkness of water on my right
to the loud blade of traffic on my left

to the double line my lover makes
toward what might lie ahead

Conditioning

High upon a hill, my heartbeats shorten;
my body stores momentum as we climb.
With sight alone I navigate the mountain—
conditioning for some up-coming time.
What draws me up the mountain is not clear,
nor the future which describes itself today.
My past counts not, no practice helps me steer;
the turns aren't mine to make along the way.
It's not my skill or bend of knee that matters
but voice and heart, and confidence is both.
And when my urgent concentration shatters,
I stay the run, pursuing movement's growth,
preparing for a time when I might need
resilient nerves, and a taste for speed.

a question of imagination

there is no touch my body
can imagine like the breezy magic you
craft

no lovelier song
than the junction of our flesh

did i play some part
in needing you
to be just what i wanted

what did i once
believe in
and
how did you hear
my breath call

Dreams of a Different Woman

What I miss most is bending
   down like wide blades, ragged
strips taped purple pink black
   to imagined drumbeats, wild waving
circles fly.

And not explaining.

What I wish most is that voice
   which climbs the perfect stairs
to every ear,
   the voice of a lusty gull,
unfit for choirs.

The notes rising through my knees.

Do you dream? they ask me. Yes,
   but not of running. Instead:
the slow scrawl my hand remembers,
   or the invisible deadly dog I cannot outrace
and must outwit.

Every night. Dreams.
   Floods. Fires. Owls. Mirrors.
Dreams not wishes, but poems.
   Every night, dreams of a different
woman.

But always, she is always me.

A Day
for Robin Stephens

A day, Robin.
Just one single day out of the future
we hope we are building.
That's what I'd give you, Robin,
give us both, if I could.

Let's make it a Saturday, and let's
arrange to be in the same state
when it happens. One day; our day.

A morning in thick down, embroidered blue, brown,
like our eyes opening.
A morning waking slowly—taking our time
to get into our chairs, and get the motors going
—not urgently,
with no demonstrations to prepare for,
because justice demonstrates itself these days;
no meetings,
which have mostly been replaced
by simple understanding;
not even a conference to attend,
because issues like caregiver abuse
and work disincentives
were settled long ago.

I'd give us
a quiet afternoon among tress, Robin,
our talk touching on cloud-shapes, goddesses,
sit-skiing and song—

not on grant writing, boards of directors,
pending legislation, mandatory access—
because in our rich, related memories,
we won.

I'd give us a monument:
the words we helped to write—
now carved in granite.
Perhaps we'd go to see it, riding downtown in a city bus
that we don't have to commandeer.

Or we'd take poles to a mountain river.
Fish surface as rain begins to fall. Huddled together
in the rain, we draw out enough rainbow
to satisfy two
stomachs and two clear minds.

Robin, the sun moves across the sky like this every day.
Watch it with me this one day.
Watch it settle into the Rockies.
And with this clear golden view
of the whole city, let's plan our evening.
I want to give us a night on the town—
yeah a night on the town!
All the hot spots and the spots
we'll heat up.
The full moon glides us
through doors opening wide to roomy tables
and rose-shaded drinks.

Large level floors rock with our dancing.
Lines form to ask for the next one
and the next one and the next one and all night long

we don't educate anybody
because that was taken care of in the last generation.

Returning home just before star-fade,
we might think into the past. We might wonder
how we carried our campaigns
into every hour;
how we poured effort, like water
down the dry throats of our sisters and brothers,
then pumped a little more
for ourselves.

And the deeper wonder:
how in the flying noise
of the days we remember living,
we came
to know each other.

REMEMBER

Remember, you're an artist, a pilgrim, a ticketed passenger, a frequent flyer. The purser's instructions, her black graceful hands sweeping red arrow nails to indicate the nearest exits, are meant for you too. You could almost recite them by now, though without the life vest demo. Remember, you're no free ride, no stowaway. You're part owner of this stale air, this scheduled departure, this defiance of gravity. You've bought your share of the exploding carbon remains that thrust steel aloft. You've let yourself be patted down and swabbed for radioactive threat. You've stowed your cell low and tight across your lap. Behind you, in front of you, and across the aisle, at least a dozen people are gripping the same lime-green novel, and you haven't even sought out a synopsis, but you can't be expected to follow every script; the pocket safety card should be enough. Remember, your taxes pay for the FAA. Remember, you're a demographic, a diviner, a modern nomad, an account. Remember, you're unabridged, strictly scrutinized, equally protected. Your personhood is legally recognized, but nowadays so is a corporation's. Remember when corporations prospered through good customer service? Remember, human nature is a myth but human rights are universal. Liability is an excuse; safety is a science. Remember to use the right lingo for each argument. Remember all the excitement when the bill was signed, the soaring promises? Remember, that doesn't apply here. Still, it's good to remember you belong here with the middle managers and the returning Disneyland disciples; you can't ask for a lot but you can ride along. Remember Bob Sampson on the Telethon? Remember who your friends are. From either left or right, if it stays clear we should be able to see the Grand Canyon. Remember, you're the seventh generation, and the keeper of one more. Remember, you're a charter member, a metropolitan citizen, a live birth, a party to the contract.

Remember, what's starting here started long ago. Remember to drink enough water. Remember what Stephen Hawking says on the tiny screen embedded in the seatback in front of you: The Universe is big, and dotted with hospitable pockets. Meteors bullet from planet to planet, pollinating ponds with twisted strands. Remember, the laws of physics never change; why should the laws of life? Remember when they used to serve real meals, like chicken with limp noodles and a side of green beans? Remember, everyone belongs to some kingdom, phylum, class, order, family, genus, species. Remember your confirmation number. Remember to breathe.

Remember, you're an evolutionary winner. Through millennia of tectonic uproar, you rose from dust deposited in primordial stew, survived ice and industrial ages, and arrived here right along with the rest of them, maybe not as erect but every bit as sapient. Your legs hang, immobile and swollen. Remember the danger of blood clots; remember to get a massage. The window seat passenger has legs exactly like a deer's, long thin and muscled, and hooved in high heels. When she climbs over yours, it's a moment of choreographed beauty.

PHOTO GALLERY

IMAGES COURTESY OF THE DENVER PUBLIC LIBRARY WESTERN HISTORY COLLECTION

p. 177, Arrest Photo, WH2274, Box 3, FF 1.

p. 178, "I was a poster child" Article, *The Disability Rag,*
September/October 1992, WH2274, Box 14.

p. 179, Publicity Photo, Ronald McDonald, Laura Hershey,
Bob Palmer, n.d., WH2274, Box 1.

p. 180, Laura Hershey Portrait, n.d., WH2274, Box 3, FF 1.

p. 181, You Get Proud by Practicing Button, WH2274,
Box 25, Envelope 2.

p. 181, Clapper, Arm Band, and Handcuff, WH2274,
Box 24, Envelope 4.

p. 182, "Barricade" Poem, 1991, WH2274, Box 4, FF 5.

p. 183, "Beats" Handwritten Poem, n.d., WH2274,
Box 3, FF 14.

p. 183, "We Weren't Carded" Poem, n.d., WH2274,
Box 3, FF 32.

p. 184, "Special Vans" Poem, 1992, WH2274, Box, 4, FF 2.

p. 185, Laura Hershey Accepting the President's Award for
Outstanding Service to America, 1998, WH2274,
Box 3, FF3.

I was a poster child

by Laura Hershey

I was a poster child. In 1973, I became a mini-celebrity, appearing at Muscular Dystrophy fundraisers throughout Colorado. I learned to smile whenever a camera appeared, and to say "thank you." I learned to look, sound, and act cute and grateful. And on Labor Day, I became a prop in the TV studio where the local portion of the Telethon was broadcast. To families, driving by to drop their contributions into a giant fishbowl outside the studio; to the camera's blinking red light; to the anchorman who squatted next to me, holding a huge microphone in my face; to everyone, I gave the same cute-and-grateful act, because that's what they wanted.

So I am no stranger to the Telethon. And in the 18 years since then, the Telethon doesn't seem to have changed much. I watched it for three or four hours last year, just to make sure. It was chillingly familiar. The sappy music, the camera close-ups of wistful faces, the voice-overs telling us about that person's dream to walk someday, the tearful stories of parents "devastated" by their child's disability, and the contributors coming forward in droves — it was all the same as I'd remembered it.

But some things have changed. I have changed. I don't know what my politics were as an 11-year-old, if I had any. But my politics now — which are not merely political but also personal, spiritual and practical — have led me to question and ultimately reject most of the values which the Telethon represents. ■

From "From poster child to protester," by Laura Hershey.

Waiting for a miracle

The telethon, says Laura Hershey, distorts reality — even in its profiles of disabled adults, which MDA always mentions as being "positive."

Just before my second year of college, I was asked to be interviewed for a pre-Telethon special. At first I said no; I was by now quite leery of the telethon mentality . . . . but the local MDA office promised the interview would . . . take a positive, realistic approach, so I agreed.

The reporter who conducted the interview in my parents' home asked good questions, and allowed me to give complete, intelligent answers. It was certainly a different process than my earlier experiences. Afterward, I felt good about the upcoming show; I had been able to discuss issues, describe my life as a college student, and project a strong, positive personality.

Or so I thought. When the program aired, my piece, through careful editing, had been turned into a sob story entitled, "Waiting for A Miracle." From that point on, I vowed to have nothing to do with the Telethon. -- L. H.

YOU
GET **P**ROUD
BY
PRACTICING

LAURA HERSHEY POETRY TAPES PO BOX 9004 DENVER, CO 80209

FREE OUR PEOPLE
ADAPT

FREE OUR PEOPLE
ADAPT

BARR▌CADE

The barricade guards this conference,
keeping safe the handsomely-dressed
indignant women and men
who walk between workshops
to talk of new markets,
avoiding liability,
and profit margins.
The barricade keeps them safe
from seeing us too clearly —
    our irregular bodies
    our flaunted freedom,
    our hand-scrawled accusatory signs —

from hearing us too loudly —
    our shouts of anger,
    our accelerating chants
    demanding "Free our People *NOW!*"
from remembering the ones back home
who look like us,
who stay hidden and do not shout,
who do not press the barricades,
whose anger instead sinks deep
into their dying hearts.

Laura Hershey 10/14/91

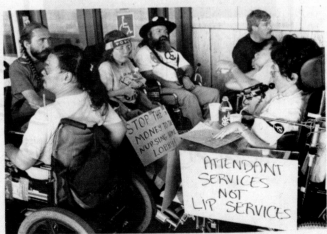

Laura Hershey (at right) and other ADAPT activists at the barricades, 1992

33

<u>**Beats**</u>

Like the beats of healthy hearts
they come
beating wings against the pull of ground:
fourteen Canada geese
filling our yard with cries of gathering ~~~~~
~~~~~~~~~~ Then they are still
~~~~~~~~~~~~~~~~~~~~~~~~~~
~~but for one or two halting struts
in the ~~late~~ November snow.
melting
And as the dusk gathers
the geese disperse:
my spirit follows one, chosen randomly,
in its up and down in space.
It climbs
the effort heats its ~~the~~
thick body farther and farther
north.
Meanwhile, my bold spirit
keeps up
but can't keep so warm
the wind blows faster
and wetter
and clouds billow and ~~~~ grab hold.
~~~~ as it crosses the ~~the~~ northern border
the goose
Drops
my frozen spirit

When we came in we weren't
carded, we rarely are, they're too
embarrassed:
For all they know
we could be sixty
or fourteen,
and either way would be a scene. We don't care, yet.
You and I both know
what doors guilt opens.

They won't guess our age
because they don't see our faces.

They see
tread tires and metal,
my bent back, your spastic arm,
the black plastic knobs that propel us.
They see the ten dollars
sent to last year's telethon; and Heidi's
spiteful cousin.

The city's renting special vans,
the daily paper reads,
The cops are getting ready,
for special people with special needs.

The mayor's special crip advisor
has given special training
in moving all our special chairs
when arresting and detaining.

They've set up special jail cells
in a building on the pier.
They've brought in special bathrooms
and nurses---never fear.

The cops are weary of our bodies
they treat us in a special way,
special smiles, if you're lucky
special brutality when you're in the way.

Bush's campaign office give us
all the special treatment we can take;
locked doors and angry words,
while Clinton's office gives us cake.

The ones who run the nursing homes
think they're doing noble deeds---
locking up our friends in cages
special people with special needs.

They put up special barricades,
to try to keep us out,
still we're in their face,
still we chant and shout.

What's so special really
about needing your own home?
If I need pride and dignity,
Is that special, just my own?

Are these really special needs,
Unique to only me?
Or is it just the common wish,
to be alive and free?

-- Laura Hershey
   10/21/92

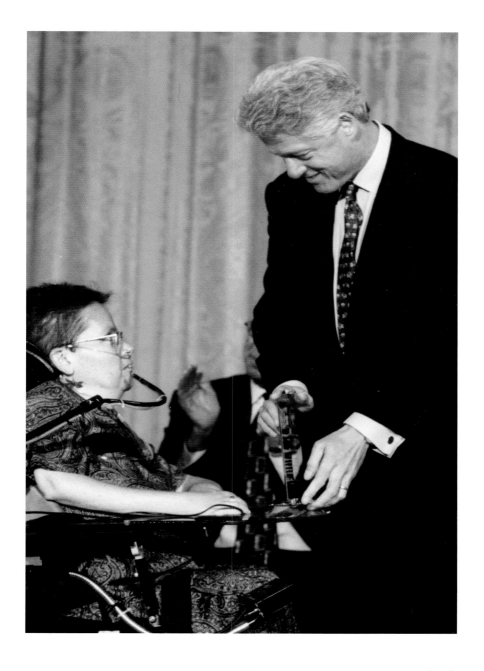

"I GO ON DECIDING ON PRIDE": WRITING AS A STAY AGAINST ERASURE IN THE POETRY OF LAURA HERSHEY

Constance Merritt

Constance Merritt received her PhD in Creative Writing from the University of Nebraska–Lincoln. She is the author of the poetry collections Blind Girl Grunt: The Selected Blues Lyrics and Other Poems *(Headmistress Press, 2017), a finalist for the 2018 Lambda Literary Award in Lesbian Poetry;* Two Rooms *(Louisiana State University Press, 2009);* Blessings and Inclemencies *(Louisiana State University Press, 2007); and* A Protocol for Touch *(University of North Texas Press, 2000), winner of the Vassar Miller Prize.*

Your parents must have felt guilty for bringing you into the world, a woman I have just met says, responding to the fact that I was born visually impaired. For a split second I am stunned, but then I think her words must be ironic, that she is mocking unenlightened ableist thought processes that devalue the lives of people with disabilities. But her words are not ironic. Rather than the elation, hope, and pride with which parents typically welcome a child into the world, she can only imagine that my parents, the parents of a "defective" child, would be riddled with disappointment and guilt.

Through her activism and through her writing, Laura Hershey insisted upon, commanded, and demanded that people with disabilities, no matter the extent of impairment, possess inherent value, and deserve not only dignity and respect, but agency and pride as well. Hershey's poems illuminate the myriad subtle and not-so-subtle erasures of disabled lives, exhort others to take up arms in the fight, and reinscribe crip lives into the world with passion, incisiveness, and grace. For Hershey, writing poetry is a form of resistance born of both psychological and existential necessity; but as vital and necessary as writing is, it is not without its risks.

In "A Call to Arms," a collection opener written in a playful, riddling tone, Hershey exhorts her readers to write poetry as a means of upending the status quo. The poem, quoted in its entirety below, begins with light bantering wordplay, but by the fourth line the diction of the poem takes on social justice overtones:

> O bark the tree; leaf the book;
> uncork the bottles, and stir the cook.
> Winter the worn, torn calendar.
> Spring the forgotten prisoner.
> Breach all borders; stoke all hopes.
> Quarter the soldier but disorder the troops.
> Draft the breeze. Beam down the sun.
> O pen your poetry, everyone. [1]

The poem moves quickly from bark to tree to leaf to book. But what does it mean to "bark the tree"? To put bark on the tree? To strip bark off the tree from which to make a writing surface— page, leaf? Or to bark up exactly the right tree as a hunting dog expertly corners its quarry? On the surface, the second line evokes domesticity, but other meanings percolate. Something has been bottled up and corked, and there will be power in the release. Think: projectile champagne corks or Molotov cocktails. The poem continues with the command to stir or stir up the cook. The third and fourth lines move logically enough from winter to its opposite spring, but then spring springs into unexpected subversive action and a call to liberation: *Spring the forgotten prisoner.* In the context of Hershey's writing and activism, the forgotten prisoner must call to mind the million plus men, women, and children shut away in nursing homes and similar institutions, as well as crip peoples generally who are imprisoned within structures and mentalities that distort, devalue, and disappear us. Hershey's life and work demanded nothing less than liberation.

The breaching of borders recalls the literal barricades contested and crossed by Hershey and her ADAPT comrades in their campaigns for equal access to public transportation, personal care attendants, and other civil rights for people with disabilities. Hershey calls on the reader to challenge all structures and institutions that keep crip peoples out of sight and out of mind, including the fictional fetish of independence. In her poems "Morning" and "Working Together," Hershey elucidates interdependence as lived experience. In "Morning," the speaker waits by turns eagerly and anxiously for the arrival of her personal care attendant, imagining reasons for her delay. In "Working Together," Hershey reveals the mutuality in the relationship between the giver and receiver of care. But even "the giver and receiver of care" misses the mark. Within the dyad of care, Hershey would have us know, there is not the one who is independent and the other who is dependent, the one who gives care and the other who receives care, but rather a mutual relationship, a dynamic dance of give and take. Through the tangle of limbs involved in a lift, and through the deeper entanglements of intimacy and empathy attendant upon relationships of care, one gains both a visceral and an intra-psychic conviction of interdependence as the ultimate reality. From this perspective, the borders to be breached are also internal, intersectional ones. In her masterful poem "Translating the Crip," Hershey writes:

> When I say *challenges to crip solidarity* I mean the
> colors missing from grant applications, the songs
> absent from laws. I mean that for all my complaints
> and victories, I am still sometimes more white than
> crip.[2]

Confronting and acknowledging how difference lives and jostles within us renders difference encountered outside of us already familiar and approachable. Confronting and acknowledging how difference lives and jostles within us likewise opens our eyes and our consciousness to the fact that privilege and oppression, power and its lack, are deeply contextual. For example, in our society, people who care for the basic bodily needs of others, from mothers to childcare workers to personal care attendants, are undervalued and underpaid. So, there is a clear power differential between the one who employs and the underpaid. Or, as Hershey points out in the lines quoted above, crip oppression notwithstanding, she is still a beneficiary of white privilege. Or, as we will see later, sometimes one identity, crip identity let's say, obscures other identities, queer identity, for example. Such awareness is necessary for any project of solidarity.

"A Call to Arms," as well as many of Hershey's other poems, such as "etc." and "Hate, But," which will be discussed later, confront the casual ableism that one encounters almost anywhere and often from those whom we imagine to be natural allies and of whom we expect more and better. The line "Quarter the soldier but disorder the troops," in "A Call to Arms," holds out hope and compassion for the individual caught in the gears of disabling mechanisms, even as it gives no quarter to disabling mechanisms in all their force and violence. In a more familiar parlance, we can honor the soldier and the veteran and still fight like hell against the war and against the military-industrial complex.

Playing off the martial diction from line 6, "draft" in the penultimate line turns the poem toward its true theme. Insofar as the breeze can't be drafted (compelled to serve), but blowest where it lists, this is an image of freedom. But the imperative may also serve as a micro craft lecture: draft (write) what is fleeting. And further: harness clarifying light ("beam down the sun"). For Hershey, inscribing one's own lived experience is a powerful act of resistance against the systems that distort, devalue, and seek to erase the lives of crip peoples, and she wants to call each of us, pen in hand, to the figurative and literal barricades.

In her ars poetica "How to Write a Poem," Hershey expands upon the micro craft lecture at the end of "A Call to Arms." Here, Hershey begins by instructing the would-be writer of poems on how not to go about the process:

> Don't use words for their own sake, or to show
> how clever you are,
> how thoroughly you have subjugated them
> to your will, the words.
>
> Don't try to write a poem
> as good as your favorite poet.
> Don't even try to write
> a good poem.[3]

Self-indulgence, cockiness, and ambition have no place in Hershey's aesthetic; a poem is more elemental and necessary than that. "Just [just!]," Hershey instructs us, "peel back the folds over your heart / and shine into it / the strongest light / from your eyes, or somewhere else."[4] Bless you, Laura Hershey, for the inclusiveness of "or somewhere else."[5] Light may come from the eyes, but it may also come from somewhere else. Wherever it comes from, again Hershey insists that illumination is one of poetry's most vital means and ends. Here she also suggests that the heart, the storehouse of personal experience and the source of life itself, is the proper source of poetry. The poem continues:

> Whatever begins bubbling forth from there,
> whatever sound or smell or color
> swells up, makes your throat
> fill with unsaid tears,
>
> whatever threatens to ignite your hair, your eyelashes,
> if you get too close—
>
> write that.[6]

These lines suggest that the poem is rooted in sensory imagery that bubbles up from the heart, emotional freight in tow ("makes your throat / fill with unsaid tears"). Whether born of joy or pain, here tears must not only be wept but spoken also. Hershey dictates that suitable poetic quarry must feel dangerous or pose some risk to the writer—"whatever threatens to ignite your hair, your eyelashes, / if you get too close— // write that." Having covered what to write, the proverbial question where do poems come from, Hershey moves on to instruct us on how to write:

> Suck it in and quickly
> shape it with your tongue
> before you grow too afraid of it
> and it gets away.[7]

We are barking (up) that same tree again, as in "A Call to Arms," trying to apprehend quarry that threatens to elude us or that just plain threatens us. Hershey urges us to breathe in or ingest the heart's flammable materials, quickly shaping them with the tongue. At its birth, the poem is utterance, a saying of "unsaid tears." And the shaping must be done quickly lest the poet lose her nerve and the quarry gets away. The final lines of the poem reprise the opening theme: poetry is not a vehicle for your ambition, but *rather it shapes itself only* to the poet's need: "Write the poem / you need to hear; / write the poem you need."[8]

In the poem "Telling," Hershey enumerates the many pitfalls encountered by crip peoples who would tell their stories. But even as she makes a full disclosure of the risks, Hershey doubles down on the imperative that we *must* tell our stories. When others' notions about you precede you and are so entrenched that they surpass the real reality of you in all your realness, showing up as yourself in the world or on the page requires nothing less than to take up arms and fight against a vast juggernaut of systemic distortions and erasures. After the opening line, "What you risk telling your story,"[9] "Telling" unfolds as a list of risks: you'll bore people; you'll embarrass yourself; you'll be misunderstood. But that's just the beginning; it gets worse:

> You will park yourself forever
> on the outside, your differentness once
> and for all revealed, dangerous.
> The names you give to yourself
> will become epithets.
> Your happiness will be called
> bravery, denial.
> Your sadness will justify their pity.
> Your fear will magnify their fears.
> Everything you say will prove something about
> their god, or their economic system.
> Your feelings, that change day
> to day, kaleidoscopic,
> will freeze in place,
> brand you forever,
> justify anything they decide to do
> with you.[10]

Even as we who lack the power to name reality, to impose meanings upon the world, and make them stick, attempt to seize power by telling our own stories. Those who possess and hoard power stand ever at the ready to overwrite and override our voices, turning tools of liberation into weapons of oppression. Because they think disability is synonymous with incompetence, we are praised for doing the least little thing. Because they think disability is synonymous with hopelessness, if we do not appear to be hopeless, we must be brave or in denial. If we should articulate negative emotions such as sadness or fear, they will lay these emotions at the door of our disability, rather than at the door of our humanity where they belong. "Everything you say will prove something about / their god, or their economic system"[11] points toward the way in which the existences of some people—crip peoples, people from non-dominant genders, cultures, classes, sexualities—are hijacked and appropriated to constitute the contents of dominant identities. We can exist to them only in so far as we can be made to *prove* some closely held notion about themselves. Though our feelings and identities may be as various as those of any human creature, we are always at risk of being frozen in place, branded forever by the unmerciful, monochromatic light of stigma. And thus reduced, we are no longer agents, but rather victims, whose stories and feelings will be made to "justify anything they decide to do / with [us]."[12] Both individually and collectively, our histories are ripe with decisions made concerning what to do *with us* and *to us* with no forethought to *consult us*. The final line of this passage pulls that awful freight in tow.

Even so, the considerable risks of telling our stories notwithstanding, Hershey insists that tell them we must:

> Those with power can afford
> to tell their story
> or not.
> Those without power
> risk everything to tell their story
> and must.[13]

As noted earlier, for those in power, reality, the world as we know it, is their story. Variations to the theme can be added, but even if not, the theme goes on humming along for its own interests. For those of us without power, our variations are off the chart, way out in no man's land where power imagines dragons. We tell our stories to create a place for being, a place where we can meet each other and thereby find ourselves. In the end, the risks of telling don't matter, because we do not tell our stories for those who will use them against us, to distort, devalue, and disappear us, but rather we tell them for each other, and for ourselves, to companion, to encourage, and to incite. As Hershey writes:

> Someone, somewhere
> will hear your story and decide to fight,
> to live and refuse compromise.
> Someone else will tell
> her own story,
> risking everything.[14]

For Hershey, telling our stories is necessary as a stay against the myriad subtle and not-so-subtle forms of erasure crip peoples face from day to day. In Hershey's poem, "the mom and pop print shop hop, or how eagles," the poet tells the story—two stories really—of such a casual, mundane act of erasure. The poem describes an encounter between the speaker and the proprietor at the mom-and-pop print shop. The poem opens with a deft scene which also doubles as an exposition of the cultural context and thematic substrate of the poem:

> how eagles
> frozen and fierce
> arched haughty judgment upon
> weaker birds that flock
> how their supposed virtue
> hung silent bronze ascension

> how engraved words
> lectured from flag spangled
> cork board walls
> how exalted main street ambition scorned the knotty
> nets of safety
> and made need a sin[15]

The positions of the proprietor and of the speaker are made clear by the imagery and diction in these opening stanzas. It also quickly becomes clear that the power and privilege of eagles underwrites how the proprietor chooses to interact with his disabled customer. In the midst of a business transaction, without so much as a by your leave, the proprietor asks the speaker if she was in an accident. While the proprietor doesn't think twice about his right to intrude upon the speaker, the speaker is caught off guard and clearly taken aback:

> how among the order specifications he
> asked
> right between 20 pound and 24 pound
> right between ember blue and ivory
> how right out of ink stained
> coffee filtered file cabinet air
> how without pardon me
> how without is this too personal
> he asked
> were you in an accident
>
> how he pressed for what to call it
> when I said all my life
> how he flickered flat lipped regret
> under eagles' yawning wings[16]

In the natural order of things, self-sufficient eagles are superior to "weaker birds that flock." Regarding the speaker with pity, in what is almost a movement toward empathy, but not, the proprietor "toss[es] off / his granddaughter's story,"[17] summing her up and dismissing her with the phrase "can't do anything" and answering the speaker's follow-up questions with "decisive negations" that enumerate what the girl can't do. Even as he admits that "oh every now and then you can see / there's something there,"[18] he dismisses this evidence of her consciousness, of her humanity, by reasserting her essential worthlessness according to the can-do criterion of eagles, "but / can't do anything."[19]

But, wait! There's more, and it's worse:

> and especially
> how he said
> *but she gets a lot*
> *of attention*[20]

Having denied his granddaughter agency of any kind, the proprietor begrudges his granddaughter the attention she receives, suggesting that despite her inability to do anything, she can somehow manipulate people into paying attention to her. Apparently, eagle logic does not have to be internally coherent. In the way that Hershey structures this poem, just telling us point by point how this happened, it is as if she is saying *I can't even*, as if the experience was too visceral and emotional to shape into coherent sentences. Experiences such as the one encountered in this poem are all-too-common experiences for people with disabilities. One minute you are going about your everyday business, feeling as though you are nothing more (or less) than an ordinary unremarkable person, and then in an instant you are confronted by someone who makes it clear that you are anything but an ordinary unremarkable human being, and you are brought up short, put back into the place where our culture and its enactors think you belong.

While disconcerting, such diminishing encounters with random strangers can be more easily shaken off, dismissed as the bumbling of a well-meaning, though thoughtless, ignoramus, than can acts of marginalization and erasure by those we believe to be our people. In her poem "etc.," Hershey describes one such experience of being marginalized by someone thought to be a natural ally. The speaker and her lover attend a bell hooks lecture where, despite the expansiveness of hooks's inclusive catalogs of different types of women, she never manages to name crip or disabled women, relegating them instead to the amorphous catch-all of etc.:

> she celebrates women
> black women women of color white women etc.
> > i am the etc.
> working class women middle class women privileged
> women
> homeless women poor and destitute women etc.
> > i am the etc.
> lesbian bisexual straight single ex- etc.
> > i am the etc.
> mother grandmother sister friend etc.
> > i am the etc.[21]

This act, this choice, is tantamount to burying crip women under a heavy shroud of invisibility. Because of the sheer expansiveness of hooks's naming, the exclusion of disabled women stands out all the more, as if she were shouting: I see, I recognize, I acknowledge all variations of the woman theme, except crip variations, nearly all women, except you and yours.

"etc." unfolds as Hershey's commentary on hooks's lecture. The layout of the poem, with hooks' words flush left and occupying most of the page and Hershey's commentary flush right and mostly hugging the page's right margin, mimics marginalia and enacts marginalization, but it also resists marginalization and erasure as Hershey is literally writing herself and her lover (and by extension crip peoples) into hooks's text. Each time hooks ends a catalog of women with etc., from the margin, Hershey asserts "i am the etc. / i am the etc. / we are the etc. / we are the etc."[22] While the poet and her lover "agree / with most of what [hooks] says / [they] both know / whom she leaves out."[23] As mammals and as humans, we all experience a deep and powerful need for belonging. In recent years, research has shown that social isolation is detrimental to both our mental and our physical health, and that strong social networks enhance almost every aspect of our lives from resilience in the face of setbacks to cognitive health to economic opportunity to rates of survival. All this to say that exclusion hurts in a myriad of tangible and intangible ways, and when encountered in places where we expect to belong, at the hands of those with whom we feel we belong, it hurts that much more.

Despite her disappointment and self-assertion, Hershey's call out of hooks is gentle, and the poem ends in a movement of admiration and reconciliation:

> bell hooks
> fierce feminist brilliant writer woman not afraid
> to dig for the root
>   etc. doesn't do her potent ideas justice
>   her critiques fit me
>   her visions fit me
>
>   but   i don't fit her words
>   except etc.
>   (i do like that term:
>   sexual practice)
>
> in practice
> sexuality seethes with meaning possibility connection
> intimacy   desire revolution   etc.
>
>   that's an etc. i can dig
>   to the root

> beside me
> your new haircut
> haloes the shape of your ear
> i think about
> kissing you
>
> etc.[24]

In this passage, Hershey expresses her admiration for and solidarity with hooks, even as she pinpoints the shortsightedness of hooks's ethical imagination—who we name or leave nameless, see or fail to see, is certainly an ethical matter. But, in what one comes to recognize as a classic Laura Hershey shift, in its final movement the poem turns its back on the agent of power, the one with the power to name or not, to include or not, to see or not, turns instead to face the intimate other, a crip woman like herself, fiercely embodied, emphatically present, and wholly desirable.

Hershey describes an experience similar to the one described in "etc." in her brilliantly incisive poem "Hate, But," however, this time marginalization of crip women by the failure to name is replaced by downright insult. The occasion of the poem is an AIDS benefit reading by *One Flew Over the Cuckoo's Nest* author Ken Kesey that Hershey attends with a group of disabled friends. But before turning to the Kesey reading, Hershey writes about her own reading earlier the same day and about her approach to public readings generally:

> But perhaps I shouldn't call it hate.
> Hate is not a word I would want to use
> in those pleasant, lavender-filled bookstores,
> those artsy cafes,
> where I have managed to capture thirty ears,
> an hour's attention,
> to build a friendly bridge of words
> between their reality
> and mine.

I have come to think of each reading
as an opportunity, a promise
of sharing, and hearing,
and seeing,
as my audience adjusts its eyes
to the appearance of my body, my wheelchair,
and opens its mind anyway.
Hate is not a word
to present to such open minds.[25]

The "friendly bridge of words" between realities that Hershey tries to build with her readings is answered in Kesey's reading with casual disregard: "the sting of unfit words— / "cripple" "inferior" "defective" "deformed" / used so easily."[26] But in the spirit of bridge-building, Hershey remains reluctant to use the word hate to describe the casual and wanton disregard for the lives of crip peoples. In the spirit of building "a friendly bridge of words," Hershey "know[s] this other word / and another, easier voice to talk about it with."[27] The other word is ignorance. But as the poem reveals, what is easy isn't necessarily what is right.

For example, one thing that is easy (or easier) and tempting, when we find ourselves the only one—Black, queer, crip—in a crowd of dominant identities, is to attempt to pass, to trade oppressed group solidarity and pride for token mascot status and quasi belonging. Confronted with the "ignorance" on display in the Ken Kesey reading, Hershey confesses:

If I were here alone, I could have overlooked it.
I could have cheered with the rest
his verbal dexterity, his colorful, inventive tale,
could have disregarded the insults,
the sting of unfit words—
        "cripple" "inferior" "defective" "deformed"
used so easily.
I could have come away from his reading
not exactly inconspicuous—

> my chair stalling a couple of times on the steep
>   auditorium ramp—
> not exactly belonging—
> exiting the building by a separate, accessible door
> but sharing the group's satisfaction, a story told well.
> But I am not here alone.[28]

"[N]ot exactly inconspicuous ... / ... not exactly belonging—" gives the lie to the siren song of passing, to the putative benefits of trading in one's own particular identity for the all-consuming embrace of the universal. Even the architecture—the steep ramp of the auditorium, the separate accessible door—underwrites inequality and maintains barriers to real belonging. Nevertheless, the fiction of quasi belonging is tempting. But Hershey is not alone. She has come to the reading with her people, with people with whom she has experienced mutuality and real belonging. Community helps us remember ourselves when others would see us as less than whole. Community helps us take pride in ourselves when others would line up to heap shame on our heads. Community emboldens us to fight for one another even as alone we would feel powerless or afraid *to fight for ourselves.*

Flanked by crip friends, Hershey is unable to overlook the ableist slurs. Gathered in the lobby "out of the crowd's way," the friends' "frustration comes spitting out." Hershey writes:

> Mary looks close to tears.
> I stare at the departing crowd,
> white Eugene liberals and their bright children.
> They are smiling six hundred smiles.
> I wonder if they would have smiled
> at a story sprinkled with "nigger" and "kike."
>
> On one thing we all agree:
> "It's just ignorance," we tell each other.
> The same old shit. The same old ignorance.[29]

Later, Hershey questions whether the author of *One Flew Over the Cuckoo's Nest* could be so ignorant, and she acknowledges that the fight against this putative ignorance is a fight that she can't win, given the smallness of her bridge-building reach, as compared to Kesey and his ilk's bridge-burning one. Hershey continues to search for the proper word to describe the structures, attitudes, and behaviors that distort, devalue, and disappear us:

> So if it is not just ignorance—
> what can I call it?
>
> What can I call the man who tells a radio host
> how glad he is
> that his daughter died young,
> because she was in a wheelchair
> and could not feed herself?[30]

My parents should have felt guilty for bringing me into the world. A man is glad that his daughter died young because she was in a wheelchair and couldn't feed herself. What can we call such attitudes, indeed, such blatant disregard for the inherent dignity and worth of disabled people's lives? "It is hard," Hershey writes, "to call it hate / without the crimes we usually associate / with hate."[31] And yet, when people refuse to see us, or use an attribute of our person as a catch-all for what's inferior, incompetent, or repugnant, they intimate or assert outright that our very being is wrong, psychically and viscerally; we experience such occurrences as an existential threat: there are people out there who believe my birth was a bad thing; a man is so glad that his daughter died young!

If, as Hershey writes, "No one has ever leaned / from a passing car / to yell at [her] clear words of hate,"[32] it is not because she has not been the object of hate, but rather because she is invisible and because the disparaging of disabled persons remains largely acceptable in polite society. In the absence of obvious evidence of hate, Hershey remains dogged, undeterred, following the scent of

her intuitive quarry to the place where the hidden face of hate is
unearthed and revealed. Hershey writes:

> They cannot imagine me being anything
> other than what
> they think they see.

> They do not know who I am,
> and this is the crime,
> this is the violence.
> This is the hidden hate
> of which I do not want to speak.[33]

As evidenced by the "but" in the title, and the desire to speak
about "ignorance," and despite her inclination to rationalize hate
away, by the final line of the poem, Hershey manages to speak
clearly and convincingly about the "hidden face of hate" that
seeks to exert enormous power over the lives of disabled people.
In "Hate, But" Hershey fearlessly and accurately names a reality
that crip peoples know and yet often do not want to know, a
reality that we feel at times with an almost unbearable intensity,
and yet shudder to call and call out by its rightful name, lest
doing so isolates us further, erodes our hope, leaving only despair.
In Hershey's poem, and in our lives, ignorance is the preferred
explanation for hateful thoughts, words, and deeds because
ignorance should be amenable to education. If hate is amenable
to anything that thing would be familiarity, familiarity borne
out of contact, proximity, and meaningful engagement. It is this
understanding that leads Hershey to assert that "this ignorance—
/ if that's what it is— / is a battle I can't win."[34] At best, her
reading has managed to overwrite vague, outdated, distorted notions
of "the handicapped" in the minds of thirty people, while Kesey
reinforces these disabling and dehumanizing notions in the minds
of six hundred with his devaluing stereotypes. The "simple math"
notwithstanding, Hershey continued, and continues through her

writing and through her example, to fight for disabled peoples—
for our dignity and respect, for our agency and pride, for our civil
rights and for our full humanity—inscribing crip lives into the
book of life with indelible ink as a stay against the myriad subtle
and not-so-subtle forms of erasure that would distort, devalue,
and disappear us.

In her poem "No Deal," addressed to voters who supported
Colorado's Amendment 2, which prohibited any constitutional
protections for LGB people, Hershey plants herself firmly in her
truth, conceding not one inch of ground to those who would have
her be anything other than the fierce, fabulous, brilliant badass
that she is:

> If you want
> my woman-self originality
> in exchange for your stern conformity
> as the price for my equality—
> I'm sorry.
> If you demand
> contrition as a necessary condition
> for acceptance
> then—
> Thanks but no thanks.
>
> This is no deal you're offering—
> this is erasure.
> But the words keep coming back.
> I go on writing my way.
> I go on making my love.
> I go on refusing your shame.
> I go on deciding on pride.
> I go on cherishing my friends.
> I go on speaking my fear.
> I go on finding my strength.
> I go on living my life.
> And you've got
> no deal. 35

NOTES

1. Laura Hershey, *Spark Before Dark* (Georgetown: Finishing Line Press, 2011), 3.

2. Laura Hershey, "Translating the Crip," Poets.org, accessed December 12, 2018, https://www.poets.org/poetsorg/poem/translating-crip.

3. Laura Hershey, *Dreams of a Different Woman: New Poems* (Denver: Dragonfly Press, 1994), 25.

4. Ibid., 25.

5. Ibid., 25.

6. Ibid., 25.

7. Ibid., 25.

8. Ibid., 26.

9. Hershey, *Spark Before Dark*, 10.

10. Ibid., 10.

11. Ibid., 10.

12. Ibid., 10.

13. Ibid., 10.

14. Ibid., 11.

15. Hershey, *Dreams of a Different Woman*, 43.

16. Ibid., 43.

17. Ibid., 43.

18. Ibid., 44.

19. Ibid., 44.

20. Ibid., 44.

21. Ibid., 39.

22. Ibid., 39.

23. Ibid., 39.

24. Ibid., 40.

25. Ibid., 36.

26. Ibid., 36.

27. Ibid., 36.

28. Ibid., 36-37.

29. Ibid., 37.

30. Ibid., 38.

31. Ibid., 38.

32. Ibid., 38.

33. Ibid., 38.

34. Ibid., 37.

35. Ibid., 45-46.

READING LAURA'S POEMS

Eli Clare

White, disabled, and genderqueer, Eli Clare lives near Lake Champlain in occupied Abenaki territory (currently known as Vermont) where he writes and proudly claims a penchant for rabble-rousing. His most recent book is the award-winning Brilliant Imperfection: Grappling with Cure.

> Inside my queer crip isolation
> your words have found seams, cracks,
> fissures—insisting, insisting: "Remember,
> you weren't the one / who made you ashamed."[1]

§

The poems of white disabled lesbian writer-activist Laura Hershey grab me, make me think about the pronoun *you*— the relationship between the *I* of the narrator and the *you* of the reader. In her well-known poem "You Get Proud by Practicing," first published in the early 1990s, Laura[2] writes directly and specifically to disabled people. There is nothing generic about the *you* in these prose-like lines:

> You do not need
> to be able to walk, or see, or hear,
> or use big, complicated words,
> or do any of the things that you just can't do

to be proud. A caseworker
cannot make you proud,
or a doctor.
You only need
more practice.
You get proud
by practicing.[3]

She is speaking to people beaten down and shamed by ableism, coaching and encouraging us toward pride. The power here lies not in a nuanced, multi-layered metaphor, nor in language honed and polished, but rather in its direct insistence that pride is powerful and attainable; the key is practice. Disability activists, particularly in the disability rights movement, have embraced Laura's poetic directives. This poem has been published at least five times, often in small grassroots publications, turned into a poster, and performed at open mic events and political rallies—the *you* Laura addresses absorbing her directives, and in turn using them to practice pride.

§

Questions about pride, queerness, and disability access hover as I read Laura's poems. I remember a conversation she and I once had about LGBTQ community. She was clear that she had found no home or resting place there. She wrote in a world shaped by the absence of ramps and elevators, which meant that all too often she couldn't access the bars, bookstores, and many other public spaces where queer and trans communities are built. She wrote in a world shaped by endless ableist stereotypes, which meant that far too many non-disabled LGBTQ people treated her as undesirable and child-like. She named the daily grind of ableism that she encountered everywhere—and felt keenly in queer community—"the violence of stairs."[4] I pause to absorb the gravity of the word *violence* and the pun on the word stairs, referring both to an architectural feature that completely privileges walking over rolling and to the act of gawking. The absence of LGBTQ pride strikes me every time I read "You Get Proud by Practicing." Throughout the poem, Laura focuses intently on disability pride:

> You can add your voice
> all night to the voices
> of a hundred and fifty others
> in a circle
> around a jailhouse
> where your brothers and sisters are being held
> for blocking buses with no lift,
> or you can be one of the ones
> inside the jailhouse,
> knowing of the circle outside.
> You can speak your love
> to a friend
> without fear.[5]

The *you* is quite specific here: disability activists protesting lack of access. I could argue that the lines, "You can speak your love / to a friend / without fear," are a veiled reference to gay/lesbian/bisexual/queer love. However, because every other image in the poem is quite straightforward, I'm not inclined to read an indirect queer meaning into these lines.

LGBTQ and disability pride are cousins, both arising from the Black Is Beautiful movement of the 1960s. Gay and lesbian activists in the early 1970s took lessons learned from Black Power activists and created the first gay pride marches, which in turn inspired disability pride parades, starting in the 1990s and becoming more numerous in the 2000s. Laura certainly participated in a number of LGBTQ pride marches, reading at the Denver event several times and speaking at the Portland, Oregon event in 1999. But in writing "You Get Proud by Practicing," she doesn't make any moves toward twining disability and LGBTQ pride together. I'm neither calling Laura out nor suggesting that as a disabled lesbian poet she had an obligation to both kinds of pride, but I do have some wonderment about her poetic choices. She and I never had this conversation, yet I yearn toward it, trying to imagine what we might have offered each other.

§

Laura—

I think about homophobia in the disability rights movement of the late 1980s and early 1990s, the casual assumptions of heterosexuality, how you and I navigated that terrain in such different ways. Friend, how did your navigations impact you and your poems? Did you simply lay that struggle down and decide to write about disability separate and distinct from queerness? Or did LGBTQ pride so inform what you understood about resisting shame that you just let it settle matter-of-factly into the background? I think too of the "violence of stairs" in LGBTQ communities, both then and now, and feel piercing anger, sadness, betrayal. I feel all of what pushed many of us—including you and me—to organize and make community among queer disabled people.

§

Yes, these questions hover, but Laura's entire body of work proclaims over the course of three decades that pride—both crip *and* queer—comes in many different forms. In "Sex," written some fifteen years after "You Get Proud by Practicing," Laura's snarky humor taps into a sensibility I associate with both queerness and the politics of pride:

We do it all the time.
We do it in so many ways.

We keep them all wondering:
What do we do? they wonder.
Straight people wonder what lesbians do.
Lesbians wonder
what disabled lesbians do.
They all wonder.

They tease us,
threaten to videotape us at night,
but they never guess,
not even when it's right
in front of their eyes.[6]

Here the narrator claims her lesbian self and her disabled self, twining them together and naming straight people's homophobia and non-disabled lesbians' ableism. Her light, bemused, self-possessed tone—"We keep them all wondering"—places queer crip identity, experience, and sexuality at the center.

I don't want to trace a simple arc between "You Get Proud by Practicing" and "Sex" or to suggest the differences between the two might reflect changes in Laura, changes in the cultural/political climate, or a little of both. Instead, I want to lay them side-by-side—two poems, one explicitly urging an entire community toward pride and the other relishing queer disabled sex:

...we do it so many ways.

Fingers. Raisins. Mouths.
Soft strong fingers, tender raisins,
open mouth.
It's easier than stopping for lunch
on the long miles between cities,
filling our stomachs and our bloodstreams
with raisins.
Your five strong fingers
organize themselves around raisins,
clumps of two or three,

push them easily into my waiting mouth.
I chew,
swallow,
taste the sugar,
then open again for more.[7]

Side-by-side, these two poems clarify that the intimate stanzas of "Sex" are also about pride—a pride held by the *we* of two lovers having disabled lesbian sex in the face of curiosity and desexualizing stereotypes. Laura sets up this political context through her snarky humor and then moves to her lover's "five strong fingers" feeding her, not an image of care—or from an ableist view point, of tragic dependency—but of pure sexiness that becomes even more overt in the next stanza: "Sweeter than raisins, / Your fingers push into me."[8] Laura whispers to me through the ether: "Remember, pride comes in many delicious guises."

2

You have made my world
more possible, words cradling, nourishing,
provoking: "When I say *tell the truth* I mean
complicate. Cry when it's no longer funny."[9]

§

Laura's poems—insistent, direct, unapologetic—keep grabbing me—inviting me to think more about the pronoun *you*. In the 2003 version of "Telling," she imagines a generic *you*, a storyteller marginalized in some way, poised on the edge of some important story. She begins:

What you risk telling your story:

You will bore them.
Your voice will break, your ink
spill and stain your coat.
No one will understand, their eyes
become fences.
You will park yourself forever
on the outside, your differentness once
and for all revealed, dangerous.
The names you give to yourself
will become epithets.[10]

The narrator is passing knowledge to this *you* about the risks of speaking through, around, over stereotypes, and the possibilities of having her words used against her.

Laura knew well the risks of storytelling. In her 2001 article "Confessions of a Cash Cow," she documents the profit Colorado home health agencies at the time made by being the bureaucratic structures through which disabled people received personal attendant services. She calculated that the agency she used raked in $32,000 per year of pure profit off of her. She writes, "I'm not a 'client.' I'm not a 'consumer.' I'm a cash cow."[11] This article was part of her on-going activism, work that ranged from changing how Colorado provided care to disabled people to organizing the 2002 Queer Disability Conference, shutting down Jerry Lewis' Labor Day Telethon to struggling against physician assisted suicide. Laura had no doubt that her public storytelling was risky. She notes in "Confessions of a Cash Cow":

> I'm not using the agency's name in this article, for a very good reason: I don't want to be "dumped." Despite the lucrative business, Colorado has few Medicaid home health agencies willing to take on "heavy care clients." I know several disabled people who have been dropped by agencies after filing complaints, or otherwise pissing them off. Some have been blackballed, ending up unable to find any agency willing to take them on.[12]

She understood the risks, not only of telling untold stories, but also of putting words on paper that could jeopardize her very survival. She faced these risks and decided to take them. In "Telling," Laura easily could have made the poetic choice to write about risky storytelling in the first person, but by using the second person, she places herself in relationship to other storytellers. In effect, she is saying, "I am not the only one taking these kinds of risks." The poem ends with an image highlighting the impact of risky stories told in community:

> Someone, somewhere
> will hear your story and decide to fight,
> to live and refuse compromise.
> Someone else will tell
> her own story,
> risking everything.[13]

As an activist and poet, she clearly valued this chain of stories and her place in it—a certain undeniable interdependency among storytellers.

§

Disability access and interdependency made Laura's writing possible. In the essay "Getting Comfortable," she chronicles the details of preparing to compose lines, stanzas, paragraphs on her computer screen. She writes:

> I just spent the past 20 minutes getting comfortable. "Move the head pillow down and a little to the right," I told Ruth, my attendant. "Push my shoulders up and to the right ... a little more. Now push the pillow down again. Straighten out my hips please." What I really wanted to do was write. First, though, I had to get comfortable. "Now could you pull my right knee to the left. More." It will be a while before another attendant

comes—which is a good thing, offering promise of some quiet time.[14]

This is the work of gaining access through care, of creating a self-determined life through interdependency. Laura names this routine with her attendant "comfort," but I want to pause to disentangle the notion of comfort from the realities of access. Marginalized peoples write frequently in conditions of great discomfort: write at kitchen tables after the dishes are washed and kids are put to bed; write after long days working a cash register or a production line, pouring concrete or waiting in line for food stamps. We write inside conditions of injustice: write from psych wards, prison cells, homeless shelters; write without enough food to eat; write when our words are trivialized, ignored, suppressed. We write through conditions of inaccessibility: write in spite of not having access to the space, technologies, relationships, and/or time necessary to put words on paper or computer screens. All these conditions—discomfort, injustice, lack of access—profoundly shape what marginalized writers write—or don't. Without access to a computer and dictation software, a microphone, an attendant to position that mic, and time to let language move from speech to text (or someone to transcribe her words), Laura's poems very well might not exist.

Laura was reluctant to write about her need for care, because she felt this story was too full of risk:

> For a long time … I have hidden the part of my life that involved the services of another woman's strong hands, arms, legs, back…. [I have] conceal[ed] the truth of the help I need in order to carry out my daily actions…. [I] gave no ground to the idea of dependency, for that's what I've heard it called in fundraising appeals and theoretical discussion…. If strangers knew about the extent to which I depend on helpers for the smallest maneuver, for relief from discomfort, and for readying

myself for any productive activity, would this not deepen their sense of my utter helplessness?[15]

She was thinking again about the hazards of writing through, around, over ableism—naming the risks but this time expressing ambivalence about taking them. Her words remind me of the persistence of shame and the power of stories and pride.

Ultimately Laura pushed through her ambivalence and made the choice she often made—to engage with the risk. In "Getting Comfortable," she asks, "If I leave behind my body to write, what (how) does the reader read? Can a reader read a mind without having a body to read?"[16] In response to her own questions, she publicly claimed her reality—her need for care. She tied the rhythm of her work with an attendant to the rhythm of her words:

> The process of getting comfortable demands a certain style, both explicatory and poetic: *You see, this is the way I want it. This is what I mean. Not quite that far. Left, not right. Pull a little further. Push again.* A careful calculation of timing, tune and tempo. This is my language: explication, correction, repetition.... Poetry *is* power of words to effect change, to move people—in this case, to move me, the author. Literally.[17]

She named her language aptly. Explication, correction, and repetition appear repeatedly in her poems over the course of thirty years. In claiming this triad, she also claimed many parts of herself all at once, inextricably linking care, access, poet, and activist together.

§

Laura—

Much of your life was made possible through
relationships—connections with personal assistants,
with your long-time partner and disabled lawyer/
activist Robin Stephens, with friends, family,
community. In an interview with you and Robin from
the early 1990s, you said: "I do need a lot of help. But
I consider myself independent.... That doesn't mean
I'm totally self-sufficient. That means I have control
over the choices I make, what I do with my life."[18] The
interviewer narrated: "Laura and Robin have found
ways to support each other.... Robin feed[s] Laura
so the two can go out to dinner unaccompanied. An
attendant used to wake Laura and turn her once each
night; now Robin does that."[19] You reflected, "And I
interpret for her in noisy environments. Or sometimes
with phone calls. She can do a lot more physically. It's
harder to see the kinds of things I can do for her."[20] The
interviewer interjected: "At this, Robin made a face of
mild impatience, an expression that said, 'Partner, you
do plenty.'"[21] Laura, I adore this exchange; I imagine
you and Robin sitting side-by-side—your love for
each other strong and vibrant—talking about the daily
realities of your self-determined lives made possible
through interdependency.

And here is my next wonderment: did you create
many different *you's* in your poems because you, who
so viscerally experienced the power of interdependency,
wanted to make your interdependent relationships with
readers transparent, direct, unwavering?

3

I am sending a whisper, a gust,
a tremoring of gratitude into the cosmos,
your words an echo: "Those without power /
risk everything to tell their story /and must."[22]

§

Laura's poems won't let go of me—*insisting*, on the "power of words to effect change, to move people."[23] This insistence ripples through her 2010 poem "Translating the Crip." Here she creates another *you*, specific but entirely different from the *you* in "You Get Proud by Practicing." This *you* Laura is ambivalent about: "Can I translate myself to you? // Do I need to? // Do I want to?"[24] This *you*, she is furious at: "When I say *nondisabled* I mean all your precious tricks."[25] This *you*, she calls out: "When I say anything I know the risk: You will accuse me of courage. I know your language all too well, steeped in its syntax of overcoming adversity."[26] At the same time, this *you*, she does not shun: "When I say courage I mean you sitting next to me, talking, both of us refusing to compare or hate ourselves."[27] Laura is unrelenting in her desire for this *you* to change—a *you* who is non-disabled, sometimes well-intentioned and patronizing, sometimes dismissive and undermining, sometimes wanting to do the work of an ally and not knowing how.

Alongside the *you* in "Translating the Crip," Laura conjures a *we*, resisting the image of herself as a lone and lonely disabled person: "By *dancing* I mean of course dancing. We dance without coordination or hearing, because music wells through walls."[28] Laura's use of this disability community *we*—much bigger than the *we* of the disabled lesbian couple in "Sex"—suggests that she was imagining multiple kinds of readers. The *you* and the *we* of the poem make me pause. I feel Laura's lines shifting between the two pronouns: "When I say *sexy* I mean our beautiful crip bodies, broken or bent, and whole. I mean drooling from habit and lust. I mean slow, slow." [29] For some readers, myself included, "drooling from habit and lust" is a common experience, and to have it articulated as ordinary, beautiful, sexy is a relief and a revelation. For others, these lines may well be startling, brand new, and unsettling, because ableism insists drooling is ugly and disgusting—the opposite of sexy. The *you* and the *we* sit side-by-side.

In the end, Laura stays focused on the non-disabled *you* in this poem. She isn't coaching and encouraging a whole community as in "You Get Proud by Practicing" or passing knowledge as in "Telling." Rather, she is engaging one-on-one, creating a demanding and clear relationship between the *I* and the *you*: "When I say *ally* I mean I'll get back to you. And you better be there." [30] The calling out of the *you* is unmistakable. But at the same time, Laura calls out herself—the *I* of the poem: "When I say *challenges to crip solidarity* ... I mean that for all my complaints and victories, I am still sometimes more white than crip." [31]

§

Laura—

Your work makes me think not only about homophobia in the disability rights movement but also about racism and whiteness. As white crips, you and I have had the luxury to ignore the rampant racism among white disability activists. That's the way white privilege works. And here's another wonderment: if you had lived longer, how would your awareness of whiteness have expanded, shifted, grown more urgent in your poetry and activism? How would disability justice—a politics that has become strong and vibrant since your death, a politics led by disabled and sick queer women and femmes of color, a politics that insists on the connections between ableism, white supremacy, capitalism, state violence, and misogyny—have pushed your work? Friend, in what ways will we as white crips rise to meet your definition of ally? I yearn to deepen our solidarity.

§

I return to Laura's poems again and again, letting their insistence, their directness sink into me. It's true that I yearn for a deepening of solidarity, a breaking of queer crip isolation, a shattering of shame. But inside Laura's words, I actually feel more promise than longing. I feel the many *you's* to whom she writes. I feel her asking us to pay fierce attention. I feel her promising us that pride in its many forms is attainable, that stories are powerful beyond measure and worth the risk, that crip bodies are broken, bent, whole, *and* sexy. I feel Laura's words, promises, poems reverberating.

NOTES

1. Laura Hershey, "You Get Proud by Practicing," *Crip Commentary*, accessed December 11, 2018, http://www.cripcommentary.com/poetry.html#PROUD.

2. Laura Hershey was a friend, a comrade, an elder of mine—an elder even though she was only months older than I—and in writing about her poetry, I find myself unable to call her by her last name. I feel none of the distance or supposed objectivity that using her last name implies. Instead, I call her by her first name, bringing with that choice an abiding familiar respect.

3. Hershey, "You Get Proud."

4. Hershey, "Translating the Crip," *make/shift*, no. 9, (2011): 44.

5. Hershey, "You Get Proud."

6. "Sex," Laura Hershey Papers, WH2274, Western History Collection, The Denver Public Library.

7. Ibid.

8. Ibid.

9. Hershey, "Translating the Crip."

10. Laura Hershey, *Spark Before Dark* (Georgetown: Finishing Line Press, 2011), 10.

11. Laura Hershey, "Confessions of a Cash Cow," *Ragged Edge* Online, no. 6 (2001), http://www.raggededgemagazine.com/1101/1101covcashcow.htm.

12. Ibid.

13. Hershey, *Spark Before Dark*, 11.

14. Laura Hershey, "Getting Comfortable"in *Beauty Is a Verb: The New Poetry of Disability*, eds. Jennifer Bartlett, Sheila F. Black, and Michael Northen (El Paso: Cinco Puntos Press, 2011), 129.

15. Ibid., 129-31.

16. Ibid., 131.

17. Ibid., 132.

18. Anndee Hochman, *Everyday Acts & Small Subversions: Women Reinventing Family, Community, and Home* (Portland: The Eighth Mountain Press, 1993), 28-29.

19. Ibid, 29.

20. Ibid.

21. Ibid.

22. Hershey, *Spark Before Dark*, 10.

23. Hershey, "Getting Comfortable," 132.

24. Hershey, "Translating the Crip," 43.

25. Ibid., 44.

26. Ibid.

27. Ibid.

28. Ibid.

29. Ibid.

30. Ibid.

31. Ibid.

UNTRANSLATABLE CRIP: LAURA HERSHEY'S POETIC LABOR TO BUILD CRIP POWER

Leah Lakshmi Piepzna-Samarasinha

Leah Lakshmi Piepzna-Samarasinha is the Lambda Award winning author of Care Work: Dreaming Disability Justice, Dirty River: A Queer Femme of Color Dreaming Her Way Home, Bodymap, Love Cake, *and co-editor of* The Revolution Starts At Home: Confronting Intimate Violence in Activist Communities. *A lead artist with Sins Invalid and the co-founder of Mangos With Chili, she is a VONA fellow and holds an MFA from Mills College.*

> Can I translate myself to you?
> Do I need to?
> Do I want to?
> —Laura Hershey, *"Translating the Crip"*

Laura Hershey is forever and a day the only white disabled writer I teach in "Frida and Harriet's Children," the online writing class by and for sick and disabled Black and brown queer writers that I've taught for four years. It's important for me to teach a class in which the participating students, as well as the writers on the syllabus, are all queer Black and brown disabled writers because of the paucity of disabled literature classes and the ways whiteness takes over disabled spaces in a hot second, and to show there is a huge and rich lineage of disabled BIPOC writing. But no one has ever complained when I teach Hershey.

I mostly teach one poem of hers, "Translating the Crip." Published before Hershey's death in November 2010, it is perhaps the last poem she ever wrote. I ask people to read it in turn, and in an exercise, we begin making a list of our own loaded, particularly disabled or sick or deaf or hoh or autistic or mad words, the words used for us and the secret words embedded in our secret disabled stories. We use her form: *when I say ___ I mean ___*. People fill in *when I say cane I mean powerful hot friend; when I say autism I mean secret precious language treasure.*

I teach this poem for many reasons, but primarily because to be a disabled writer is to grapple with the ways language has been used to define and erase us: heroic, inspirational tragedy, the disclosure of the body's terrible sad secrets as the only disabled story. As Hershey says in the next-to-last knockout punch of her poem:

> When I say anything I know the risk: You will accuse
> me of courage. I know your language all too well,
> steeped in its syntax of overcoming adversity and limited
> resources. When *I say courage* I mean you sitting next
> to me, talking, both of us refusing to compare or hate
> ourselves.[1]

Hershey knows all too well nondisabled language is abled language, and how killing it is. Abled language doesn't even know it's "abled language"—it just thinks of itself as language. How boring. Here is this whole entire multiverse apart from "overcoming adversity and limited resources."

And all of it starts with *I.* The repetition Hershey chooses brings a staccato, compelling rhythm to her poem. It is also an important political choice that she punctuates it with *I.* When *I* say. *I* mean. As I was writing this essay, I needed to look at the text of the poem again—was *you* ever in the poem, in the way of: "When *you* say disabled, *you* mean...." And it wasn't. Phrasing a poem that way, as in "when you (person with privilege) say this thing about me, you do this violent thing and you are an asshole," is something that happens often as a format in protest poetry. It calls out the oppressor for doing wrong. It's not wrong, it goes over great at a slam, and I've used that strategy. But in making that choice, the oppressor is still centered, even if they're centered as the jerk. In "Translating the Crip," Hershey makes a subtle yet powerful alternative poetic choice—the disabled *I* is always centered, is always the one speaking. And not to the oppressor first or only or primarily, but to other disabled people.

Hershey's poem, and her canon, is a deep flipside of the "let me explain disability to the abled, or call out the abled while still focusing on them. Her poetic choices are focused on lifting up, unapologetically, all the secret, beautiful, incomprehensible and deeply understandable sick, disabled, mad, deaf, and neurodivergent languages we hold—secret languages of our hands and bodies. "Incomprehensible" crip tongues that editors insist there is no market for, and no history of, and thus no need. They ask us to explain and explain the secret inside of the world where we communicate our own way to them. Hershey shows disabled languages without translating them for the abled—she celebrates and explores them for ourselves. She leaves many things unexplained, in a disabled space. As the social media world becomes more and more the panopticon—personal data mined for capitalist dollars, expectations of us being visible in perfect ways at all times to be able to economically and socially survive, spying so present we take it for granted, friends turning their trauma stories into brand for dollars—something I think a lot about is the power of the unseen, what's not on Facebook or Instagram, what is below the radar, what they can't see coming or spy on and is powerful in that inability to be turned into a target market. Our disabled bodyminds' languages are a weapon in that space. Hershey's poetry is an exploration of all the ways we are incredibly and always powerful, even and especially as the abled world refuses to witness us.

And, there is the tender and potent crip moment of solidarity, of turning courage on its ear, when Hershey says:

> When *I* say *courage* I mean you sitting
> next to me, talking, both of us refusing to compare or
> hate ourselves.[2]

I called my next book of poetry *Tonguebreaker* for a reason. When I started envisioning it, I was planning on writing about the ways Sri Lankan names and words are "too long" and unpronounceable by white tongues—and how this is used against us; but it is also about the way we hold our spaces while locked out of power. As I kept writing, I wrote more pieces about how disabled language and bodyminds are persistently incomprehensible to the nondisabled. We are slow, stupid, ungainly. The nondisabled refuse to learn ASL, or slow down to listen to our adaptive communication, watch our fingerspell, pain face, our clear articulation of what we are and need. We also have power. Here power is private—is hidden in what the nondisabled don't understand.

Hershey's poem "Translating the Crip" follows that initial, powerful set of questions about translation with a couplet that embodies crip power:

> When I say *crip* I mean flesh-proof power, flash
> mob sticks and wheels in busy intersections, model mock.[3]

Look what she does there. Power. Internal crip language that a nondisabled person may not comprehend, but we are right there with her in that wheelchair and scooter-led ADAPT protest. The alliteration and fast paced consonance of *model mock*. We're right there "stuck" in that intersection, an inconvenience that becomes power, in the speed and slow excitement of disabled protest.

Here's the other thing: I didn't know Hershey. I didn't know who she was or her two decades of disabled queer radical literary and political work. I didn't know a damn thing about her before she died. I had been neurodiverse since birth and sick since the age of twenty-one at least, probably earlier, but in the spoken word/poetry program I studied in at college, my teachers didn't teach disabled writers, or name disability as part of the lexicon of identity and power. Or if they did, those works missed me. Disability writers aren't taught, and so even when invested and involved as activists, we miss out on knowing our lineage. I read Audre Lorde's *The Cancer Journals* and tried to pass my copy on to my mom. But did anyone speak of disabled poets, disabled activism, or disability wisdom as worthy of being articulated through a disabled lens? No, they did not.

So, it was 2011, almost twenty years later, when I found Hershey's work. I was performing with Sins Invalid, the life giving disability justice performance collective, for my second show with them. We had just done the epically unheard of disabled act of postponing our big fall 2010 show to April 2011, when our director got seriously ill and confronted multiple struggles with or in the medical industrial complex. In the performance world, one way that ableism embeds itself is that "the show must go on" and there's never any option to cancel or reschedule a performance for cripness, so we end up present only physically. Except, we did cancel and reschedule, Sins did, and we wrote about it as a political act of cripping performance. The show went on, on crip time, five months later, which of course allowed the show to get even deeper and more wild and present and all the things no one tells you are brilliant about this artful disabled way of life. So I was all up in Sins for an extra six months of rehearsing, rewriting, hanging out, being at the show for tech week, hanging in the crip time machine we made of paper mache and in that community.

Hershey passed on November 28, 2010. Like many people, including those in the crip community, we got word of her passing in the early months of 2011, when I was deeply in that Sins space and in between far too many jobs and struggles with the ableism of the community. I searched and found a memorial invitation emailed to the Sins family with apologies if this was the first time we'd heard of her death. I saw collective members gasping in grief and disbelief that she'd gone. And, when I looked at my Facebook friend requests, there she was. She'd asked me to be her friend and I hadn't known who she was, so I hadn't said yes. And she'd passed before we met each other. This shook me. And started me thinking, a lot about how as disabled people we are kept from knowing each other in so many ways. We are kept from connecting because of being locked in institutions and inaccessibility, because of Access-a-Ride failures and chemical exposure meltdowns. We are also kept from connecting because one or both of us don't think of ourselves as that word. We are kept from knowing each other because we lack a cultural container of disability culture, poetics, activism, and love.

I wrote a poem about this titled, "Where would I find you," in which I talk about the places disabled people find each other, the places I was starting to find other crips: in an elevator, (working or not) on BART, in fights on Facebook about the need for access information, where the disabled and nondisabled play roles—the disabled ask for access to events and the nondisabled are in disbelief at such requests, and folks get angry. Then there is the slow/walking lane at the Berkeley Y pool and my friend's house with its ramp and all its couches—all sites for potential revolution and connection. And in the poem, I mention I had yet to come across Hershey and her work until after she died.

Death, and meeting people after death, hanging around close to death, and being familiar with it, are all crip places. And perhaps one crip poetics place is coming across someone's work after their death, and after ableism has kept you from hanging out, when you were both were alive and doing work from that same place.

Hershey was unapologetic in her work and did whatever the hell she wanted. I'm sure she struggled with shame and internalized ableism and homophobia and trauma and the ableist bullshit of editors and the publishing industry like we all do. In many ways, her writing trajectory reminds me of some things I find awesome and similar in June Jordan's career. Jordan also wrote whatever the hell she wanted, spanning genres from poetry to opera to essays for *The Progressive* to a young adult novel written in Black English about safer sex. Jordan fought like hell with editors (the editors at Routledge, for her genius poetry curriculum, *Poetry for the People: A Revolutionary Blueprint,* apparently wanted something a lot more tame), and the phone company to not cut her off utilities, and her bosses at UC Berkeley to pay for her cancer treatment. Both Hershey's and Jordan's lives are disabled queer writing lives, in white and Black, where the writers are virtuosic in the space they cover in the face of a lot of bullshit.

In reading through some of the enormous archive of her work, I see that Hershey wrote whatever the hell she wanted, and wrote about disabled experiences without dumbing them down or making the experiences simple, comprehensible, easy. In the prose poem "nights," she writes a crip landscape of fighting to lose her virginity, carefully planning her attendant's overnight and an Access-a-Ride trip, only to discover her queerness in her lack of sexual response to her cis male partner's body. That night leads inexorably to a night where she meets her queer lover in a giant crip protest of inaccessible transit in suburban Detroit. The details do not translate anything for the nondisabled. They tell a common, relatable disabled queer sex story, in all its complex mashup of sex denied and fought for, by, and through, ableism— the crip spaces of booking one way Dial-A-Rides, her partner hissing, asking if she is 'proud to turn on a man like that,' and her discovering of her queerness through that clashing:

It should be perfect, this carefully planned event. It took all week to arrange it: You phoned Dial-A-Ride twice, first scheduling a one-way wheelchair van trip from your flat in London to his (they knew the way, of course, he's a regular customer too) and then hanging up and calling back to schedule another one-way trip, the next day, from his to yours. As if they wouldn't figure out that it's an overnight stay. And who cared if they did. Dial-A-Ride customers need sex too.

Then you spoke with your attendant, Margie, delicately explaining that you needed her to work right through, 2 p.m. Wednesday to 2 p.m. Thursday, to go with you to his flat, and then you would arrange for her to have some time off later Thursday afternoon and evening. You would be having dinner, breakfast, and lunch there, sleeping there ... Margie got it. Your blushing was unnecessary but unavoidable.

It should be perfect, this long-awaited chance to lose the virginity you were beginning to think you'd be stuck with forever. You're already composing a letter to your high school friend Cam who beat you to it, who gloated when at last she convinced her gay friend Michael to give her a go. You'll announce that you too are now officially *not* a virgin though of course you officially *are,* still, because nothing has happened yet, except that it *is* happening, something is happening, right now, and that's what seems to be the problem. It isn't perfect.[4]

I'm writing this piece the week of the Brett Kavanaugh hearings, which have unleashed an ocean of survivor stories and also conversations about the politics of sharing our stories. Thinking through the politics of writing and sharing our stories of being sexually, physically, and emotionally abused, writer and transformative justice organizer Ejeris Dixon wrote powerfully about the dangers of creating a dichotomy between "brave activists" who share their stories and the "quiet traumatized survivors" who hide in the shadows. It's just another iteration of "good survivors" versus "bad survivors." Dixon goes on to say: "While I deeply believe in the power of sharing our stories and am in full support of the courageous ways that people are sharing their survivorship, stories alone will not end violence or rape culture. Our movements are created by a web of strategies, stories play a part, and there's room for all of us."[5] I agree, and add that I believe the idea of the "broken survivor" to be deeply ableist.

But in both cases, I think there is an undeniable power in telling our disabled and survivor (and both) stories without making them simple or pretty or neat or quick. There is power in telling our truths. Telling our truths through the layers of ableist and survivorhood denying shame is not simple. In her 2007 interview with *Feministing*, when asked what most people think about disability, Hershey responds, "I think the main thing is that people think of [one's disability] as a private little problem, a tragedy. They don't think it has anything to do with the world."[6] Most people can barely handle the dull basics, let alone the complex disabled and survivor thundercloud of our crip trauma genius. And the politics of getting this published are even more problematic.

I don't know the inside story of Hershey's writing career, of whether she struggled with editors and publishers or not. But I do see, in looking at her long writing career, how her poetry chapbook was published by a print-on-demand press many of my friends have used when no one would publish them and how her words are found here and there—in *Drunken Boat*, in small lit mags, and on her blog, on public radio talking telethons, about buses and assisted suicide, in an interview on *Feministing*. And still, she is less likely to be taught in feminist, queer poetics classrooms. I want to know that story—the story of how she made a decades-long queer, disabled writing life in the 1990s and 2000s. I want to know that story so I can add and share it and teach it in my archive of models and tactics for how to be a disabled queer writer.

Because we are all improbably miracles—not the kind the pitying nondisabled mean. But it is a miracle that we are here, so many of us, disabled, deaf, sick, crazy, and neurodivergent, Black, brown, queer, and poor, in the teeth of the beast called Amerika, writing goddamn poetry about our lives.

The way we got here is not an accident. It is a bunch of specific and interlocking crip stories about what tactics and hustles and community sweat make our poetry possible. And how do we find each other? How do we choose when and where we translate and when our words speak in their own crip or sick or mad or autistic or deaf languages without translation or apology to one other? Hershey was and is part of a disability justice poetics movement that—similar to feminist, queer, trans, fat, Black, brown, and other oppressed communities' poetics—has at its foundation the work of writing for each other in our own rhetoric, without assuming a nondisabled audience.

I found her work after her death, but our queer crip poetics means we keep speaking to each other, because the worlds of alive and dead aren't as far away as the nondisabled think. We know better. I mean the way my autistic poetics uses echotextia[7] as a poetic strategy to animate the lineages of crip poetics I call on, when I reference her words "I mean slow, slow." In my piece "crip sex moments"—riff and echotext crip/autistic refrain, not rip off, as one old not friend once accused me of. And that brings me to one of my favorite stanzas, which is:

> When I say *family* I mean *all* the ways we need each
> other, beyond your hardening itch and paternal
> property rights, our encumbering love and ripping
> losses. I mean everything ripples.[8]

Hershey having left the world is a ripping loss, the kind of crip loss that makes our love so encumbering—because we don't know how much time we have together or alive in the same time. It continues to be a miraculous rarity for disabled kin to be in the same room at the same time. Sometimes we don't know what to do with that gift when it happens. Often, we do. And because this life is not promised—because of progressive disability, the violence of the MIC and the police and our families, the ways we endure or embrace isolation, and more—our love is more real than the nondisabled, to me. Hershey's work reaching to me and me reaching back is a crip poetic technique of blurring the line between ancestor and living bodymind. We work together—alive and dead, archive and present day poets—to create a disability justice poetics where we are each other's reference point, best thing, point of debate and discussion; where we *"tell the truth* [and] complicate. Cry when it's no longer / funny."[9] Where the colors are not absent from grant applications, the songs not absent from laws, where white crips can admit without crying that for "all [their] / complaints and victories, [they are] still sometimes more white than crip."[10] And where the movement itself is far from almost all white and crip.

Hershey's poetic choices are one big assertion of a fundamental piece of crip knowledge—that since our bodies are already illegal, we gain nothing from making our stories simple, palatable, easy for the nondisabled to digest. Her poetic labor built so much of the groundwork for what we may be building now—an intersectional crip poetics that refuses to simplify our poems and literature and stories for someone else's convenience.

NOTES

1. Laura Hershey, "Translating the Crip," *The Violence of Stairs* (blog), March 6, 2012, http://theviolenceofstairs.tumblr.com/post/18862318185/translating-the-crip.

2. Ibid.

3. Ibid.

4. Laura Hershey, "Nights," *Drunken Boat*, Slant/Sex #2 Folio (web magazine), August 2011, http://www.drunkenboat.com/db14/5sex/intro.php.

5. Ejeris Dixon, Facebook post, https://www.facebook.com/ejeris.dixon/posts/10215517652747729, September 30, 2018.

6. Celina de Leon, "Laura Hershey: Disability Rights Activist Extraordinaire," *Feministing* (blog), January 26, 2007, http://feministing.com/2007/01/26/laura_hershey_disability_right.

7. Echolalia is an autistic communication strategy where words or phrases are repeated, often "copied" from another's speech, written text or vocal speech. Echotextia is a word I coined several years ago to describe my own autistic poetic form of conversing with and refraining other poet or writers' words.

8. Laura Hershey, "Translating the Crip."

9. Ibid.

10. Ibid.

"YOUR TIRE MARKS THROUGH THE PETUNIAS": LAURA HERSHEY'S QUEER, CRIP ECOPOETICS

Declan Gould

Declan Gould holds an MFA in poetry from Temple University and is a doctoral candidate at the University at Buffalo. She is the author of the chapbooks "Like" or "As" (dancing girl press, 2017), Model Figure *(Shirt Pocket Press, 2015), and the co-editor of* (Dis)Integration: Buffalo Poets, Writers, Artists 2017. *Her writing appears or is forthcoming in the* Journal of Literary and Cultural Disability Studies, Amodern, Denver Quarterly, P-Queue, Full Stop, The Conversant, *and* Jacket2.

Attempts to "rehabilitate" queer and disabled people are often presented by religious and medical authorities as ways of returning the nonconforming individual to a "natural" state. As Douglas Baynton writes in "Disability and the Justification of Inequality in American History," "The natural and the normal both are ways of establishing the universal, unquestionable good and right. Both are also ways of establishing social hierarchies that justify the denial of legitimacy and certain rights to individuals or groups."[1] In a gesture that pushes against these traditional conceptions of nature as an expression of the normal, Laura Hershey liberates nature from the service of heteronormativity in order to explore the potential of nature imagery to investigate queer, crip experience. Hershey's poetry uses nature metaphors to explore her experiences and theories of queer, crip romance and resistance.

As a poet who came of age in the 1980s and used a powerchair, Hershey's writing would have been subject to several stereotypes. During the mid to late 20th century, the few responses to poetry by writers who use wheelchairs that actually addressed disability (rather than leaving it out altogether) were dominated by reductive ways of talking about the relationship between disability and writing. The assumption that disability is a source of suffering and isolation dominated the discourse, and within this framework, critics tended to interpret hopefulness and positivity in writing by poets who used wheelchairs, such as American poet Vassar Miller and Irish prose writer Christy Brown, as evidence of their presumed social and physical isolation and their courageous ability to overcome the "tragedy" of disability.[2] This refusal to consider disability experience in any way that conflicts with the assumption that it is reducible to pain and suffering reveals just how radical Hershey's explorations of nature metaphors for queer, crip romance and resistance were at that time.

My analysis of Hershey's poetry is informed by Tanya Titchkosky and Amy Vidali's theories of disability metaphor, Anthony J. Nocella's eco crip theory, and Alison Kafer's queer crip theory. Vidali argues for an unsettled approach to metaphor as a technique that can open up ways of thinking about illness and disability that disrupt and rethink ableist assumptions. This "disability approach to metaphor" shifts "disability away from something only "used" or "represented" by metaphor. Instead, disability interprets, challenges, and articulates metaphors."[3] Similarly, Titchkosky argues for the "creative potential of *metaphor.*"[4] As she advocates in "Life with Dead Metaphors," rather than "killing the metaphors," the task should be "to stop putting a lid on our capacity to imagine a different world."[5] Along with building on Titchkosky and Vidali's suggestion that poets and critics alike should acknowledge the potential that metaphors for disability have to be productive as well as damaging, my analysis of Hershey's poetry also builds on Nocella's observation, as paraphrased by Ray and Sibara, that "disability studies' critiques of normalcy and its valuations of interdependence" are in sync "with theorizations of ecology."[6] While Nocella's notion that both ecology and disability studies embrace "interdependence and diversity" implicitly pushes against the common wisdom that disability and environmentalism are inherently at odds, an assumption that is based largely on the idea that people with disabilities need more resources to stay alive than nondisabled people, Kafer's "imagined futures" pushes against the assumption that queer people should reject the concept of futurity due to its coercively heteronormative underpinnings.[7] Instead, Kafer argues that "[t]he task then, is not so much to refuse the future as to imagine disability and disability futures otherwise, as part of other, alternate temporalities that do not cast disabled people out of time, as the sign of the future of no future."[8] As my analysis will show, although Hershey's poetry preceded Kafer, Nocella, Titchkosky, and Vidali's theories by about 20 years, in many ways her work anticipates their theories and the larger debates in which they intervene.

QUEER, CRIP RESISTANCE

Published in Hershey's 1994 chapbook *Dreams of a Different Woman*, "Delving" uses mining and oil drilling imagery to describe a male hospital technician's attempts to draw her blood, an experience which in turn develops into a metaphor for the intersecting violence of medicine, heteronormativity, and patriarchy. This oil drilling/mining imagery is first suggested in section i of the poem:

> Wearing white,
> technicians come bearing trays
> of needles, syringes; each tries
> to locate the rich, secret
> vein, running deep in my bent arm.[9]

Initially, Hershey resists the phallic needle wielded and the violent medical and patriarchal systems that it represents, screaming "a child's futile rage, protective of my swaddled seam."[10] But when the technician "withdraws the clumsy lance," she begins to consider the consequences that not allowing him to draw her blood might have, tells him to "start again" and becomes "[r]econciled to the search."[11] This resignation turns to active encouragement when she "urges / the tiny honed spear toward its mark" and then confesses her inability to "map" the vein "for the awkward drill."[12] The poem ends with a couplet that leaves Hershey pondering "which side I am on / of these fought and delving searches."[13]

While the shift from opposition to reconciliation, from encouragement to complicity, may initially seem to suggest that "Delving" is ultimately ambivalent about the heteronormative, medical violence represented by the needle, a closer look at Hershey's nature imagery suggests an alternate reading. Throughout the poem, Hershey portrays the needle—and by extension the technician and the hospital—as "cold,""clumsy,"and indifferent, comparing the needle not only to an "awkward drill," but also to a "clumsy lance" and "clean metal spearing flesh."[14] In contrast, she likens her veins not only to a precious natural resource, such as gold or oil, and a "swaddled" baby, but also to menstrual blood, a "cache of riches, potent red life," and a "ruby wellspring."[15] In other words, in "Delving," Hershey associates the needle/hospital with violence and exploitation and the vein/

precious natural resource with abundance, potential, and vitality. This contrast reveals that although Hershey documents a moment of ambivalence about her role in the medical system, ultimately her language inscribes its brutality, and creates the oppositional relationship at the center of this poem as a self-evident image of violence perpetrated by medicine or patriarchy and resistance enacted by a disabled queer body. The question of her complicity is a passing one that pales in comparison to the wider systemic context of undeniable heteronormative, medical violence.

Like "Delving," Hershey's poem "Sentence," published in *Shakespeare's Monkey Review* in 2009 (and in the chapbook *Spark Before Dark*, edited by Leah Maines and published a year after Hershey's death in 2010), contrasts the vitality of queer, crip resistance with the oppressiveness of heteronormative social systems. However, "Sentence" is more abstract than "Delving," and uses a series of associations to evoke these oppressive systems in lieu of investigating how they manifest through any particular institution, such as medicine. For example, Hershey imagines that her words are perceived by many as "overdue / overstaying welcome," and pictures them "mocking man's grid-block calendar / overpainting the lines."[16] These words are a:

> red banner spreading silk   message of
> time passing
> cradle rocking   falling
> power   blood   speaking.[17]

She goes on to declare that "control / is out of the question / period,"[18] suggesting not only that the message of change and of a new kind of (female) power cannot be suppressed, but will take a form that will likely be perceived as excessive and disruptive when measured by traditional standards. In contrast, the images of calendars and lines create a sense of rigidity and prescriptiveness, suggesting that these qualities are inherently exclusionary.

An opposition between the inflexible narrowness of calendars or lines, the oppressive structures that they represent, and the inclusive and the unruliness of nature develops over the course of "Sentence." Hershey establishes this opposition first by comparing the process of speaking or writing to "an easy birth" and her words to "graceless eloquent tissue" whose "force" she reveres and respects, despite her lack of concern about where her "issue lands."[19] Hershey presents the image of this easy, almost casual birth to this powerful, articulate infant as a natural, even beautiful, scene, comparing her bodily fluids to "petals" scattering and describing the infant as "roseflesh."[20] In addition to associating the act of a disabled queer woman's speaking/writing with the generative biological process of childbirth, this metaphor also suggests that Hershey views her words as precious; like a child, they are permanently tied to her, a part of her, but also capable of leading lives of their own. This sense of unbridled potential is also evoked by the extended larva or butterfly metaphor that closes the poem where Hershey imagines her words as a larva that "palpitates free of this nutritious enclosure."[21] The "shocking colors" of this insect as it "takes flight" echo the impression created earlier in the poem that despite the natural beauty of her words, they are still a message of resistance, and will therefore be perceived as excessive and disruptive by many."[22]

While Hershey opposes the wildness of nature imagery with the violence of manmade objects in "Sentence" and "Delving," in "Petunias," the image of an orderly flowerbed becomes a metaphor for the temptation to choose the pleasures of private life over taking political action, and the personal sacrifices that such action involves. "Petunias," which was published in Hershey's 1992 chapbook *In the Way*, speaks directly to Hershey's partner, and confesses to having second thoughts about her planned civil disobedience arrest as she watches her:

> ...[drive her] chair
> around a cop,

up a hill,
through careful, distinctly unrevolutionary
petunias,
past a police barricade.[23]

Hershey imagines that if she were to call her partner back and convince her to "forget the cause," then she would be able to "pick some petunias, / and take [her] home."[24] As enticing as this thought is, Hershey promptly reminds herself that she and her partner would likely not have a shared home to return to without "this clash" and the mutual sacrifices they have both made—and continue to make—for the sake of "the movement." Hershey's account in the following stanza of imagining this "small insight" as "a hand-picked bouquet" that she would have liked "to offer" her partner may suggest that Hershey is not entirely convinced by this logic. On the other hand, this stanza could also be read as Hershey's way of beginning to let go of her desire for the pretty but overly domesticated petunias, as she instead imagines an even more valuable offering. This internal conflict is reinforced by the closing image of "your tire marks through the petunias," which could be read as a sign of Hershey's lingering regret, or as a sign of their defiant triumph over the overly orderly, objectionably conventional petunias.

QUEER, CRIP ROMANTIC KINSHIP

By using nature metaphors to investigate both romantic relationships and sociopolitical resistance, Hershey suggests that they are two sides of the same coin. Although she acknowledges the tensions that arise between investing energy into public versus private life, ultimately political resistance makes queer, crip erotic relationships possible. These romantic relationships in turn enact resistance to the oppression of queer and/or disabled people. For example, in "canyon," published in *Spark Before Dark*, Hershey offers readers an extended metaphor for sex with the narrator as the imagined "banks" or walls of the canyon and her lover as the "river" that runs through it. By providing an inclusive, accommodating way to articulate her experiences with queer crip love and eroticism, the nature imagery in "canyon" allows Hershey to investigate the fluidity and creativity of the relationship between her and her partner. For example, she writes:

> I deepen   with every gush
> widen or   narrow to hold your eddies
>
> your circuitous   irresistible current
> your slow melt   and your occasional
> delightful   rapids.[25]

Here, the images of the water's flux and the canyon's constantly changing topography suggest that the two partners are constantly changing, constantly responding to one-another's changes. Fluidity is also embodied in the form of the poem, which invites readers to experiment with reading across the caesuras, which visually mimic the image of a meandering river, versus reading straight down the (albeit uneven) columns of text. This poem concludes with Hershey's assurance that even "if some summers   the river / seeps a dusty trace my shores unwet / still   the canyon lives."[26] Here, Hershey suggests that although it may not be apparent to others, part of the canyon's— and this relationship's—value lies in its fluidity and the unique kind of creativity that this experience with mutability engenders.

As with "canyon," in "etc." Hershey uses nature not only to express sensuality, but also to explore her experiences with romantic relationships and the implications that these experiences have for queer crip individuals and communities more broadly. "etc" begins with a critique of how a speech she is attending given by bell hooks "leaves out" disabled women.[27] Hershey observes that even though hooks is a "fierce feminist brilliant writer woman not afraid / to dig for the root,"[28] she fails to acknowledge that most of the ideas in her speech fit disabled women, too. These observations are intermingled with a series of rueful variations on the phrase "I am the etc.," which come to a head at the end of the poem, where Hershey reflects on hooks's concept of "sexual practice," stating:

> in practice
> sexuality seethes with meaning possibility connection
> intimacy   desire   revolution   etc.

>   that's an etc. i can dig
>   to the root

>   beside me
>   your new haircut
>   haloes the shape of your ear
>   i think about
>   kissing you

>   etc.[29]

In this second iteration, Hershey's use of the phrase "dig to the root" shifts from being a dead metaphor for the act of deep intellectual analysis to a literalized metaphor whose sensual imagery of earth and organic matter becomes revived and eroticized in the context of Hershey's thoughts about her partner's sexual attractiveness. Along with the sexualization of "etc" in the last line of the poem, this playful reanimation of the nature metaphor "dig to the root" complicates the fit/misfit, in/out binaries evoked earlier in the poem, suggesting that while the problems that hooks's speech—and (black) feminism more broadly—pose for disabled women remain, by shifting her focus onto her relationship with her partner in the midst of this politically charged event, she and her partner are able to inject a moment of solidarity and even pleasure into an otherwise alienating event.

While a revitalized nature metaphor serves as the hinge between critique and creating a sense of connection and pleasure in "etc.," the nature metaphors in "Insomnia" help Hershey develop a theory about the meaning of the differences between two people in a relationship. Published in *Wordgathering* in 2010, and collected in *Spark Before Dark*, "Insomnia" begins by comparing the "grudge" she holds onto after she and her partner have had an argument to "a pea of gravel stuck / in our sock-like fit."[30] While Hershey continues to "hold tight to hurt / slicking it to pearl," she notices that for her partner, "sleep has already / softened the stone to nothingness."[31] Initially the gravel metaphor is Hershey's way of articulating how, in light of both their closeness and interdependence, something as seemingly small as a grudge can become a source of real anguish. But, noticing that her partner has already managed to fall asleep, she considers another possible way of interpreting this metaphor—that under the right conditions, it does not take much time at all for a piece of stone or a grudge to become worn down and reduced to the point of insignificance. This leads her to the additional revelation that holding "tight to hurt" might also, ironically, have the potential to produce something valuable; that over time she may be able to turn this feeling into something else entirely. In the next stanza, Hershey adds a second divergence to the one established in the first stanza. After an evening of satisfying sex, the rhythm of her partner's breathing keeps her awake, while this same rhythm seems to lull her partner to sleep. In the third stanza, Hershey describes how their limbs touch as they sleep, and how these overlaps create temporary connections. In the final stanza, she reflects on the possibility that the thoughts running through her mind while her partner sleeps beside her, like "pages" stirred and "poems uncollected," are what make their relationship work. These final lines suggest that the insights she has gained from reflecting on their relationship—in part through the use of nature metaphors—over the course of the poem have led her to the conclusion that rather than being a source of division, the differences between her and her partner (Hershey's insomnia versus her partner's deep sleep, Hershey's stewing versus her partner's letting go) may actually be what keep their relationship "alive," in the sense that they keep the relationship from becoming apathetic, rote, or static.

Laura Hershey develops many of her crip understandings of kinship, romance, and resistance through nature metaphors rather than through inherited norms. As Eli Clare writes in "Stolen Bodies, Reclaimed Bodies: Disability and Queerness":

> The work of refiguring the world is often framed as the work of changing the material, external conditions of our oppression. But just as certainly, our bodies— or, more accurately, what we believe about our bodies— need to change so that they don't become storage sites, traps, for the very oppression we want to eradicate. For me, this work is about shattering the belief that my body is wrong. It began when I found communities committed to both pride and resistance. It was there that I could begin to embrace irrevocable difference."[32]

Hershey's explorations of her experiences with and theoretical approaches to queer crip romance and resistance rewrite heteronormative discourses about femininity, family, and kinship. She uses nature metaphors to fashion different kinds of relationships and social orders (instead of reproducing familiar ones), proposing models for creative kinship that are based on nonreproductive family building and nonreproductive eroticism as retellings of her lived experience and reclamations of her queer disabled body.

NOTES

1. Douglas Baynton, "Disability and the Justification of Inequality in American History," in *The New Disability History: American Perspectives*, eds. Paul K.

Longmore and Laurie Umansky (New York: New York University Press, 2001), 35.

2. Steven Ford Brown, ed., *Heart's Invention: On the Poetry of Vassar Miller* (Houston: Ford-Brown & Co., 1998), 19-21, 48-49, 63-64, 123, 135, 152.

3. Amy Vidali, "Seeing What We Know: Disability and Theories of Metaphor," *Journal of Literary and Cultural Disability Studies* 4, no. 1 (2010), 42.

4. Tanya Titchkosky, "Life with Dead Metaphors: Impairment Rhetoric in Social Justice Praxis," *Journal of Literary and Cultural Disability Studies* 9, no. 1 (2015), 1.

5. Titchkosky, "Life with Dead Metaphors," 16.

6. Sarah Jaquette Ray and Jay Sibara, "Introduction," in *Disability Studies and the Environmental Humanities: Toward an Eco-Crip Theory*, eds. Sarah Jaquette Ray and Jay Sibara (Lincoln: University of Nebraska Press, 2017), 9.

7. Ray and Sibara, "Introduction," 9.

8. Alison Kafer, *Feminist, Queer, Crip* (Bloomington: Indiana University Press, 2013), 34.

9. Laura Hershey, "Delving," *Dreams of a Different Woman* (Denver: Laura Hershey, 1994), 13.

10. Ibid., 13.

11. Ibid., 13.

12. Ibid., 14.

13. Ibid., 14.

14. Ibid., 13-14.

15. Ibid., 13-14.

16. Laura Hershey, "Sentence," *Spark Before Dark* (Georgetown: Finishing Line Press, 2011), 23.

17. Ibid., 23.

18. Ibid., 23.

19. Ibid., 23.

20. Ibid., 23.

21. Ibid., 23.

22. Ibid., 24.

23. Laura Hershey, "Petunias," *In the Way* (Denver: Dragonfly Press, 1992), 23.

24. Ibid., 23.

25. Laura Hershey, "canyon," *Spark Before Dark*, 15.

26. Ibid.

27. Laura Hershey, "etc.," *Dreams of a Different Woman*, 39.

28. Ibid., 40.

29. Ibid.

30. Laura Hershey, "Insomnia," *Spark Before Dark*, 12.

31. Ibid.

32. Eli Clare, "Stolen Bodies, Reclaimed Bodies: Disability and Queerness," *Public Culture* 13, no. 3 (2001), 363.

NOTES & ACKNOWLEDGEMENTS

EDITORS' NOTES

MEG DAY is the 2015-16 recipient of the Amy Lowell Poetry Travelling Scholarship, a 2013 recipient of an NEA Fellowship in Poetry, and the author of *Last Psalm at Sea Level* (Barrow Street 2014), winner of the Publishing Triangle's Audre Lorde Award, and a finalist for the 2016 Kate Tufts Discovery Award. Day is currently an Assistant Professor of English & Creative Writing at Franklin & Marshall College. www.megday.com

NIKI HERD is the author of *The Language of Shedding Skin*, which was published as part of the Editor's Select Series for Main Street Rag. Her poems have appeared in *Obsidian*, *The Rumpus* and *North American Review*. Her work has been supported by the Cave Canem Foundation and the Bread Loaf Writers' Conference. She is pursuing her Ph.D. in Literature and Creative Writing at the University of Houston, where she is an Inprint C. Glenn Cambor Fellow.

ACKNOWLEDGEMENTS

FROM MEG DAY: This volume would not have been possible without the generosity of Robin Stephens, whose patience and guidance helped shape this homage long before I approached the Unsung Masters Series. Thank you, Robin, for being willing to let me collect our kin and honor Laura in this way. I extend my gratitude to Kevin Prufer, Wayne Miller, Kate Nuernberger, and the Unsung Masters Series Board for lending their support in making this volume possible. Thank you especially to Kevin for seeing the necessity for and impact of this poet in the series; I appreciate every effort you've made toward accessible conference calls, lunches, and editions of this text. To Niki, a thousand thanks: I am so grateful for your comradery, tireless labor, patience with my schedule, and the great relief of working alongside—and being in difficult conversation with—kin. I raise my hands in praise to Eli, Declan, Leah, and Constance. You have shown me new ways of reading Laura and reminded me again and again: nothing about us without us. This project came alive with the help of the unflappable staff at the Laura Hershey archive housed in the Denver Public Library's Western History Collection. Thank you for pursuing alongside me some difficult requests and for tending Hershey's archive with such care. My heart to Jillian Weise, who met me there and has helped me tend, too, what Hershey's legacy means for disabled poets and beloveds alike. And to the original nine poets on the land at Lambda—Oliver Bendorf, Jaime Shearn Coan, Gina Evers, Douglas Ray, Christopher Soden, Julie Weber, and Valerie Wetlaufer—thank you for never straying too far in joy or in grief.

FROM NIKI HERD: Many thanks to Kevin Prufer and Meg Day for the opportunity to be part of this project. Meg—thank you for your editorial guidance and generosity. A special thanks to the Unsung Masters Series Board, especially Wayne Miller and Jenny Molberg, for support and assistance, and Sarah Ehlers, for the archive. Much gratitude to Martin Rock for his patience and design expertise; and to Christian Bancroft and Paige Quiñones for their support at various stages. Thank you to the University of Houston Department of English—to J. Kastely and Andre Cobb for making the trip to Hershey's archives possible. And gratitude to Nancy Luton for making this important work possible.

This book is produced as a collaboration
between Pleiades Press and
Gulf Coast: A Journal of Literature and Fine Arts
and
Copper Nickel

GENEROUS SUPPORT AND FUNDING PROVIDED BY:

Cynthia Woods Mitchell Center for the Arts
Houston Arts Alliance
University of Houston
Missouri Arts Council
University of Central Missouri
National Endowment for the Arts

This book is set in Adobe Caslon Pro type
with Ostrich Sans Inline and Dense titles.

Designed and typeset by Martin Rock.